WOMEN CHOSEN
FOR PUBLIC OFFICE

WOMEN CHOSEN
FOR PUBLIC OFFICE

Isobel V. Morin

The Oliver Press, Inc.
Minneapolis

Library of Congress Cataloging-in-Publication Data

Morin, Isobel V., 1928-
Women chosen for public office / Isobel V. Morin
p.   cm.—(Profiles)
Includes bibliographical references and index.
ISBN 1-881508-20-X
1. Women in public life—United States—Biography—Juvenile
literature. 2. Women government executives—United States—
Biography—Juvenile literature. 3. Women judges—United
States—Biography—Juvenile literature. [1. Women in public
life. 2. Women—Biography.] I. Title. II. Series: Profiles
(Minneapolis, Minn.)
HQ1391.U5M67 1995
920.72'0973—dc20
[B]   94-22097
                                           CIP
                                         AC

ISBN 1-881508-20-X
Profiles XV
Printed in the United States of America

99 98 97 96 95   8 7 6 5 4 3 2 1

Contents

State Department Chief of Staff P. F. Allen swears in Ruth Bryan Owen, the first woman to serve as a U.S. ambassador.

Introduction

*T*hroughout much of U.S. history, women were not allowed to vote or hold public office, and most people believed that women were not suited to handle the world of politics and public affairs. However, being excluded from official government activities did not keep women from participating in politics. Women took part in a variety of informal political activities, from raising funds on behalf of political causes to lobbying public officials to influence their decisions.

Even before the start of the twentieth century, women supported reforms to improve working conditions and to help the poor, the sick, and the elderly. Despite their ineligibility to vote or to hold elective office, some women were appointed to public offices during this period.

The adoption of the Nineteenth Amendment in 1920 guaranteed women the right to vote. After that time, women increased their share of appointive offices at all levels of government. Their numbers were still relatively small, however, when compared to male office holders. Moreover, many appointments were to positions that either carried no real power or were to areas of government that seemed related to women's traditional role as caretakers of their families and homes.

During the 1930s, President Franklin Roosevelt stepped up the pace of women's participation in politics by naming several women to important positions in the federal government. Roosevelt appointed the first woman cabinet member, the first woman to head a diplomatic mission to a foreign country, and the first woman judge to a federal appeals court. In the years that followed, other U.S. presidents appointed women as cabinet secretaries, judges, ambassadors, and members or heads of countless government commissions.

Sixty years after Roosevelt took office, women continued to make significant strides in government. In 1993, President Bill Clinton named women to several important federal offices, including Janet Reno as the first woman to become the U.S. attorney general and Ruth Bader Ginsburg as the second woman Supreme Court justice.

This book looks at nine women who have held appointive offices in the federal government, including

Dorothea Dix, who held an unpaid appointment as superintendent of army nurses during the Civil War, and Julia Lathrop and Mary Anderson, who both received important positions in the U.S. Department of Labor.

One chapter of this book profiles Ruth Bryan Owen Rohde, the U.S. ambassador to Denmark during the 1930s and the first American woman to lead a diplomatic mission overseas. Two chapters feature women cabinet members: Frances Perkins, the first woman to hold a cabinet appointment, served as U.S. secretary of labor under President Franklin Roosevelt, and Patricia Roberts Harris, who headed the Department of Housing and Urban Development and became the first black woman appointed to a cabinet position. Finally, three chapters highlight women judges: Florence Ellinwood Allen, the first woman to serve on a U.S. Court of Appeals, Constance Baker Motley, the first black woman appointed as a federal judge, and Supreme Court justice Ruth Bader Ginsburg.

Although the appointment of women to high-level government offices still generates considerable publicity, lower-level appointments often pass without much attention to the fact that the new officials are women. Perhaps one day women will receive presidential appointments as often as men—and perhaps one day a woman will decide such appointments.

Dorothea Dix (1802-1887), one of the first women appointed to a position of authority in the U.S. government, earned international respect as a social reformer.

1

Dorothea Dix
Superintendent of Army Nurses

*I*n 1867, the editor of *Godey's Lady's Book*, one of the first successful magazines for American women, asked Dorothea Dix to provide information about herself for an upcoming book about the lives of distinguished women. The editors had decided to include Dix because her impressive efforts to improve living conditions for the mentally ill had made her one of the best known women in the United States. A zealous crusader, Dix's soft voice and genteel manners masked an iron-willed determination. Throughout her life, she confronted the nation's wealthiest and most powerful men at a time when American women were not encouraged to participate in political affairs.

Dorothea Lynde Dix, the first of Joseph and Mary Dix's three children, was born on April 4, 1802, in a frontier village near Bangor, Maine. The Dix family had not approved of Joseph's marriage to Mary Bigelow because she was considerably older than he. Moreover, Joseph's family thought that Mary's manners were unsuitable for a member of a cultured family.

Nevertheless, Joseph's father, Elijah Dix—a successful physician and land developer—tried to help the newlyweds by putting Joseph in charge of his extensive land holdings around Bangor. Joseph Dix, however, was not cut out for a business career and instead decided to make a living as a traveling preacher. Dix supplemented his modest preacher's earnings by selling religious books, which his family stitched together by hand.

Because of her mother's poor health, young Dorothea had many responsibilities while growing up. In addition to the usual household chores and the book-stitching, Dorothea took care of her two younger brothers, Joseph Jr. and Charles. Only occasional visits to her father's parents in Boston relieved Dorothea from her bleak life at home. Elijah Dix showered his granddaughter with affection, so his death in 1809 left Dorothea missing him very much.

12

When Dorothea was 12, she grew frustrated with her home life and decided to live with her grandmother, Dorothy Dix. Her grandmother was determined to teach the youngster proper manners, but young Dorothea—who had spent much of her childhood caring for her brothers—was not used to taking orders from anyone. Her grandmother solved this problem by sending Dorothea to Worcester, Massachusetts, about 40 miles west of Boston, to live with other relatives.

Once Dorothea moved away from her domineering grandmother, her behavior gradually improved. Dorothea enjoyed living in Worcester, where she had young cousins for companionship and plenty of things to do. By the time she returned to Boston in 1819, Dorothea Dix had acquired the cultured voice and dignified manner that she displayed for the rest of her life.

Shortly after returning to Boston, Dorothea persuaded her grandmother to let her open a small primary school in the Dix mansion. At that time, many educated women supported themselves in this way. Dedicated to her work, Dorothea seldom engaged in the social activities enjoyed by many of Boston's wealthy young people. At a time when other young women were concerned with "catching" a good husband, Dix spent her time teaching and studying. Perhaps her broken engagement to a second cousin, Edward Bangs, made her turn away from what she considered to be frivolous activities.

This strenuous work load soon took its toll on Dorothea Dix. Her persistent cough worried her doctor, who recommended that she take time off from work to rest. Unable to teach, Dix wrote religious meditations, poems, and stories for children. After recovering her health, Dix started another school in 1831. But again her health suffered. In 1836, on her doctor's advice, she traveled to Liverpool, England. There, she spent 18 months living with some of her doctor's friends.

While she was in England, however, both her mother and her grandmother died. After returning to the United States in 1837, Dix was still too physically drained to resume teaching. Dix was restless and lonely until she found her lifelong calling to crusade for humane treatment of the mentally ill.

In March 1841, Dix offered to help with the religious instruction of the women inmates at a local jail. On her arrival at the jail in East Cambridge, Massachusetts, she found that a few of the inmates appeared to be mentally ill. Dix was shocked by the sight of these women, filthy and shivering in unheated quarters, and she immediately asked the jailer to provide heat for them.

The jailer replied that "lunatics"—a term commonly used at the time for the mentally ill—didn't feel the cold. Outraged by the jailer's insensitive response, Dix complained to the local court about the poor conditions she had found. She also enlisted the help of two influential

Residents of "insane asylums" were often neglected and mistreated during the nineteenth century, when few people were trained to care for the mentally ill.

Bostonians: Samuel Gridley Howe, who had pioneered education for children with visual and hearing impairments, and Charles Sumner, who later served in the U.S. Senate. After these two men confirmed Dix's report on the jail conditions, the jailer agreed to improve living conditions for the mentally ill inmates.

Dix's experience at the East Cambridge jail prompted her to learn as much as she could about mental illness. At that time, few people knew the causes of mental illness or how to treat it. Some people believed evil spirits caused this illness, while others believed that God

Massachusetts senator Charles Sumner (1811-1874), who served from 1851 to 1874, strongly supported the abolition of slavery and other reforms.

punished sinners by making them mentally ill. Although there was growing support for the establishment of institutions designed to care for the mentally ill, few of these institutions existed in the United States during the early nineteenth century.

Many people suffering from mental illnesses spent their days in prisons and poorhouses. Jailers often chained or whipped the mentally ill or subjected them to other forms of cruel treatment. Sometimes, public officials boarded other mentally ill people with local residents, who would feed and house them at a low cost to the taxpayers.

Dix's early studies convinced her that Massachusetts needed to do more for its mentally ill residents. Actually, Massachusetts provided better treatment for the mentally ill than many other states at that time. In the 1830s, Horace Mann, an educational reformer who helped to establish the U.S. public elementary school system, had persuaded the state to open two institutions for the mentally ill. But these institutions, then called "insane asylums," were unable to care for the sizeable number of mentally ill people in the state.

After discussing the matter with Mann, Howe, and Sumner, Dorothea Dix decided she needed more facts about the problem before she could recommend a solution. Visiting every jail, prison, and poorhouse in Massachusetts, Dix saw firsthand how the inmates lived, and she took extensive notes on her findings. By the time she completed an 18-month investigation, Dix believed she had enough evidence to convince the state legislature of the need for action.

On her return to Boston, Dix compiled the results of her research in a written petition, called a memorial. Howe presented the "Dix Memorial" to the Massachusetts legislature in January 1843, providing shocking details on the dreadful conditions under which many of the state's mentally ill lived. The critical report identified both the institutions that mistreated the mentally ill and the public officials responsible for their care.

Horace Mann (1796-1859), who in 1853 became the first president of Antioch College in Yellow Springs, Ohio, helped to pioneer the idea of co-education, with men and women taking courses together.

The "Dix Memorial" produced a storm of protest both from public officials and from ordinary citizens. Who was this woman, people demanded, and why was she poking her nose into places where no respectable woman should go? Howe, Sumner, and Mann took Dix's side in the ongoing public debate, and Dix defended her findings through correspondence and personal meetings with legislators and local officials. The four reformers—one woman and three men—gradually convinced the public and the legislators of the need for improvements in the state's treatment of the mentally ill. As a result, the legislature voted to spend more money to improve the living conditions for the mentally ill in state institutions.

Elated by her success in Massachusetts, Dix tackled the problem of care for the mentally ill in other states. For the next several years, she traveled across the United States by stagecoach, farm wagon, steamboat, railroad, and—if necessary—on foot. Everywhere she went, Dix examined conditions in public institutions. Then, she assembled her findings and petitioned state legislatures to make changes.

In each state she visited, Dix tried to convince the public of the need for institutions to house and help the mentally ill. Because taxes were never popular, Dix understood the wisdom of building public support for a reform in addition to convincing lawmakers to spend public money on it.

A shrewd bargainer, Dix usually asked for more than she expected to get. She learned to classify the state legislators into groups: 1) those most likely to favor her proposals, 2) those most likely to oppose them, 3) those whom she could persuade to change their minds, and 4) those most likely to influence other lawmakers' decisions. Dix then met with the legislators alone or in small groups at various locations. At these meetings, she used a mixture of detailed evidence and persuasive skills to win over the legislators. Her efforts resulted in the establishment of 32 state mental institutions throughout the eastern United States.

Encouraged by her success in dealing with state legislatures, Dix tried to persuade the U.S. Congress to give federally owned land to the states for the construction of mental hospitals, but her efforts were unsuccessful. The U.S. Congress had already given land for the states to build schools and railroads.

Between 1848 and 1854, Congress defeated Dix's bill several times. If the bill passed in one house of Congress, the other house would vote it down. Finally, in 1854, the House of Representatives *and* the Senate passed the bill—but President Franklin Pierce vetoed it. He maintained that Congress had no authority to make grants for charitable institutions outside of Washington, D.C. Despite a long, bitter debate, the congressional supporters of the bill failed to get the necessary two-thirds majority that would be necessary to overturn the president's veto.

Frustrated by the failure of her six-year effort, Dix sailed for Europe in September 1854. There, she spent the next two years touring the British Isles and the European continent, investigating the care of the mentally ill and pushing for improvements where needed. Her efforts during that period helped to persuade many nations to establish institutions for the care of the mentally ill and to improve those already in existence.

When Dix returned to the United States in the autumn of 1856, the growing controversy over slavery was threatening to tear the country apart. Dix avoided expressing an opinion on this heated issue, however, because she did not want to offend potential supporters of her crusade for better treatment of the mentally ill. Because she remained uninvolved in the slavery debate, Dix generally received a warm welcome in both northern and southern states during this difficult period.

After the start of the Civil War, Dix temporarily abandoned her crusade for the mentally ill. She believed that her experience working with hospitals for the mentally ill would be useful in arranging for the care of wounded Union soldiers who were fighting Confederate troops from the seceding southern states. Dix offered to

The War Between the States began on April 12, 1861, when Confederate forces bombarded Fort Sumter, a federal military base located outside of Charleston, South Carolina. The fighting would continue until 1865.

recruit nurses for this work. On April 23, 1861, Secretary of War Simon Cameron accepted her offer to select and supervise women nurses, and Dix was commissioned the superintendent of women war nurses on June 10 that year. This was the first time a woman received a federal appointment in the United States.

Her efforts to organize the work of caring for wounded soldiers caused difficulties for Dix, however. Her authority over the women nurses overlapped with that of the army doctors and the U.S. Sanitary Commission, a new group of civilian volunteers who worked to provide medical supplies for wounded soldiers and to improve sanitation in military camps and forts. This overlap in jurisdiction soon resulted in a battle of wills. She antagonized many army doctors by insisting that they abstain from alcoholic beverages. In addition, she tried to persuade the army to discharge any doctor she caught drinking on duty.

The persuasive skills that had made Dix such a successful advocate on behalf of the mentally ill deserted her when she tackled the military and civilian officials in the federal government. Dix, who was nearly 60 years old when the war started, had grown accustomed to getting her own way. She was often rigid and uncompromising in her dealings with the army doctors and the members of the U.S. Sanitary Commission. Also, many of these men resented taking orders from a woman.

Refusing to delegate authority to others except when absolutely necessary, Dix insisted on personally approving the selection of every nurse under her supervision. She also established what many people thought were unfair and unreasonable standards for the nurses. Dix insisted that the nurses be between 30 and 50 years old, and that they dress modestly in brown or black dresses with no ornaments, frills, or jewelry. Dix rejected any applicants who appeared to be looking for adventure. She told her nurses they had better be prepared for hard work, not fun!

To curb Dix's demands, Secretary of War Edwin Stanton (who had replaced Cameron in 1862) issued an order that sharply limited Dix's authority over army nurses in October 1863. Hurt and angry, Dix considered resigning, but she stayed on the job until after the war ended in 1865.

Upon her return to civilian life, Dix resumed her visits to hospitals, poorhouses, and prisons, but her health was failing. In 1881, she retired and decided to move into an apartment in the state mental hospital in Trenton, New Jersey, which she had helped to establish in 1848. She died there on July 18, 1887. Almost 100 years later, in 1983, the U.S. Postal Service issued a stamp bearing Dix's image, a tribute to her pioneering efforts on behalf of the mentally ill.

While working for the Department of Labor, Julia Lathrop (1858-1932) insisted that the government take special measures to protect children.

2

Julia Lathrop
Director of the U.S. Children's Bureau

*B*y the end of the nineteenth century, reformer Dorothea Dix had drawn public attention to the problems facing people who suffered from mental illnesses. But patients in mental hospitals were not the only ones suffering from neglect and mistreatment. The elderly, the disabled, and orphaned or abandoned children also frequently fell victim to society's unthinking or uncaring attitude. Americans needed another crusader to remind them of their obligation to care for those least able to care for themselves. That crusader was an affluent mid-western woman named Julia Lathrop.

Julia Lathrop, the first of William and Sarah "Adeline" Lathrop's five children, was born on June 29, 1858, in Rockford, Illinois, about 85 miles west of Chicago. William Lathrop, a successful lawyer who had helped to organize the Republican Party in Illinois in 1854, served in both the Illinois legislature and the U.S. Congress. The Lathrops were reform-minded people who supported the growing movements to end slavery and give women the right to vote.

After graduating from Rockford High School, young Julia enrolled in the Rockford Female Seminary. Her mother had been a member of the seminary's first graduating class. Julia stayed at the school only a year before transferring to Vassar College in Poughkeepsie, New York. (Vassar, now co-ed, had opened in 1865 as the first women's college in the United States.)

During Julia's senior year, her sister, Anna, joined her at Vassar. The two women were fortunate because, in those days, many women were not able to attend college. Even fewer had the money or support to attend college more than 900 miles away from home.

After she graduated from Vassar in 1880, Julia Lathrop returned to Rockford, where she did secretarial work for her father and two local manufacturing firms. Like her parents, Julia was concerned about social issues. However, she became a reformer only after hearing two former Rockford Seminary students speak. The two women—Jane Addams and Ellen Gates Starr—spoke about their plans for living and working among Chicago's poor.

In 1890, 32-year-old Lathrop joined Addams and Starr in their work at the Hull House, a settlement house in Chicago that the two women had opened in 1889. (The settlement houses in poor city neighborhoods were places where middle-class reformers lived while trying to help their impoverished neighbors.)

Jane Addams (1860 -1935), who helped to found the Hull House, received the Nobel Peace Prize in 1931 for her lifelong dedication to helping the poor and disadvantaged.

Julia Lathrop's move to the Hull House gave her a firsthand look at the everyday miseries faced by the people in Chicago's crowded slums. Lathrop and the other Hull House residents struggled to provide practical help for their neighbors and searched for ways to eliminate the social conditions that led to poverty.

Impressed with Lathrop's work on behalf of Chicago's poor, Governor John Altgeld appointed her to the Illinois State Board of Charities, which supervised the state's public charitable institutions. (Lathrop was the first woman ever named to the board.) Except for a brief interval in the early 1900s, Lathrop served from 1893 until 1909, when the board was replaced by a state agency with a paid staff.

As a member of the Illinois State Board of Charities, Lathrop investigated the conditions at poorhouses and other charitable institutions in the state. Like Dorothea Dix had done in Massachusetts more than 50 years earlier, Lathrop personally visited all the public charitable institutions in Illinois. During her visits, she inspected the buildings and facilities, and she talked to the residents, employees, and supervisors.

While traveling throughout Illinois, Lathrop sometimes rode in a farm wagon or waded through muddy areas to reach the orphanages, "insane asylums," which housed the mentally ill, and "poor farms," which were public institutions that housed and employed impoverished people. Lathrop found shocking conditions at these institutions. Children, the elderly, the sick, and the mentally ill often shared living quarters. Moreover, they often endured poor food, inadequate heat, and cruel treatment.

These problems existed because many of the people in charge of these institutions were political appointees who knew little about social issues. Additionally, some of these administrators were more interested in raising their own salaries than in serving the needs of their residents. Angered and saddened by what she saw, Lathrop pushed for better training for institutional workers and a civil service system to replace political appointments. She suggested that patients in mental hospitals engage in hobbies or useful work instead of sitting idle all day. Lathrop also recommended opening outpatient clinics and training families to care for mentally ill loved ones so more people with mental illnesses could live at home.

Because she was a firm believer in promoting greater public knowledge about the nature and treatment of mental illness, Lathrop became a charter member of the National Committee for Mental Hygiene. Clifford Beers, a former patient at an institution for the mentally ill, had founded this organization in 1909 to educate the public about mental illness. Such education was badly needed because public knowledge about mental illness had not advanced much since Dorothea Dix's time. Many people still believed that this type of illness was a sign of moral weakness rather than a disease that had nothing to do with how religious or ethical someone was.

After writing
A Mind That
Found Itself, *an*
autobiographical
account of his
confinement in a
mental institution,
Clifford Beers
(1876-1943)
convinced doctors to
try harder to treat
and prevent mental
illness.

Another area of public concern at this time was how to deal with children who committed crimes. In the late nineteenth century, no separate courts or prisons existed for juvenile offenders. Still, judges hesitated to send young offenders to prisons, which were intended for adults and where youths would encounter hardened criminals.

As a compromise, judges sometimes sent juvenile offenders to live in industrial schools, which were designed for youths and where young offenders could learn useful trades. Many people, however, thought this solution was not entirely satisfactory because the offenders might corrupt the other students, who were mainly neglected or orphaned children with no criminal records.

These children, pictured during the early 1900s, attended the North Bennett Street Industrial School in Boston.

Faced with this dilemma, judges often freed young offenders, even after they had repeatedly broken the law.

Because such methods of dealing with juvenile offenders seem blatantly inadequate to Lathrop, she persuaded the state of Illinois to establish the world's first juvenile court. Lathrop hoped that the court would help children who committed crimes to correct their behavior and grow into responsible adults. Lathrop also persuaded the state to establish a psychiatric clinic for young offenders who had mental or emotional problems. In addition, the state set up a juvenile detention center so juvenile offenders would not have to live with adult criminals.

Through her work in Illinois, Lathrop discovered that poverty, crime, overcrowding, poor sanitation, and inadequate disease control, as well as a lack of recreational facilities and educational opportunities, were commonplace in large cities. Moreover, infant mortality was high in both urban and rural areas, and children who lived past infancy often suffered from poor health.

Like Lathrop, other social reformers across the United States became aware of these problems and began to push for the establishment of a federal agency to deal with the needs of infants and children. In 1906, sympathetic members of the U.S. Congress introduced a bill to establish a national children's bureau. But the bill did not initially pass, in part because many people feared that such an agency would pry into their private lives.

Nevertheless, the supporters of the bill persisted, and in 1912 Congress established the Children's Bureau as part of the U.S. Department of Commerce and Labor. (The following year, when Commerce and Labor became separate departments of the federal government, the Children's Bureau moved to the Labor Department.)

On June 4, 1912, President William Howard Taft named Julia Lathrop the first director of the Children's Bureau, and she held that post until 1921. The appointment was a significant milestone for U.S. women. For the first time, a woman was in charge of a federal agency with the authority to spend tax money.

The new agency initially had little money to spend. With its small staff and budget, the Children's Bureau

President William Howard Taft (1857-1930), who held office from 1909 to 1913, thought so highly of his wife Nellie's political skills that he once sent her a note addressed to "Mrs. Taft—the real president from the nominal president."

had to choose its projects carefully. Lathrop, therefore, initially focused on the effort to reduce infant mortality. During its first two years of existence, the bureau produced and distributed free pamphlets on the health needs of pregnant women and the care of infants. These pamphlets were often a young woman's only source of reliable information about pregnancy, childbirth, and the care of newborns.

In 1917, Lathrop recommended that Congress provide financial aid to states for programs to reduce both infant and maternal mortality rates, which were still high in spite of the efforts of the Children's Bureau. Another pioneering woman, Jeannette Rankin, who had recently become the first woman ever elected to the U.S. Congress, introduced a bill in the House of Representatives to provide such aid. However, because opponents claimed that such government meddling would destroy the family, the bill failed to pass.

The advocates of federal aid to states for maternal and child welfare continued their push for legislation. Because of this, Congress passed the Sheppard-Towner Act in 1921. This act established grants to provide states with health care for mothers and infants.

After the Sheppard-Towner Act became law, the controversy over these grants continued. Disturbed by the establishment of a Communist government in Russia in 1917, many Americans worried that something similar might occur in the United States. Moreover, the

Reformer and pacifist Jeannette Rankin (1880-1973) was the first woman elected to the U.S. Congress. She held office from 1917 to 1919 and again from 1941 to 1943.

American Medical Association called the new law an "imported socialist scheme," and opponents accused Lathrop and other women who supported the act of being part of a sinister "spider's web" of Communist conspirators. Many people began to believe that Lathrop and others meant to destroy traditional American institutions.

Despite the strenuous efforts of the law's supporters, Congress discontinued the maternal and child health grants in 1929. Six years later, during Franklin Roosevelt's presidency, the Social Security Act included a new grant program to help the states provide maternal and child welfare services.

During her nine years as head of the Children's Bureau, Lathrop ardently supported federal action to regulate child labor, which she regarded as a serious social problem. In those days, many children worked long hours with unsafe factory equipment or in dangerous mines, and permanent job-related injuries and illnesses were common among child workers. With the support of the Children's Bureau, Congress passed laws in 1916 and 1919 to regulate child labor. The U.S. Supreme Court, however, struck down both laws because the justices believed that Congress had no constitutional authority to regulate the work done by children.

The opponents of child labor then pushed for a constitutional amendment to give the federal government this authority. After her retirement from the Children's

During the early twentieth century, children often injured themselves while working long hours with factory equipment that had been designed for adults.

To earn money for their families, many boys endangered their lives in the early 1900s by assisting coal miners.

Bureau, Lathrop campaigned for this proposed amendment, which Congress passed in 1925. The amendment never became part of the Constitution, however, because it failed to receive approval from three-fourths of the state legislatures, which is a necessary step to amend the U.S. Constitution.

Subsequent events, however, removed the need for a child labor amendment. In 1938, relying on its power to regulate interstate commerce, Congress passed the Fair Labor Standards Act. This law included provisions that regulated child labor in industries involved in interstate commerce. In 1941, in *U.S. v. Darby*, the U.S. Supreme Court unanimously upheld the 1938 law. Today, both federal and state laws regulate children's work.

In the years following her retirement from the Children's Bureau, Lathrop became active in the League of Women Voters, which had been formed in 1920. Lathrop served as president of the league's Illinois chapter and served on the board of its national organization. Lathrop, who remained active in both national and international attempts to improve children's living conditions, was also a member of the Child Welfare Committee of the League of Nations from 1925 until 1931.

One of Lathrop's last crusades was an effort to save a young murderer from dying in the electric chair. Russell

Carrie Chapman Catt (left) leads an early meeting of the League of Women Voters, which she helped organize to increase women's involvement in politics.

McWilliams, who shot and killed a streetcar operator during a robbery in August 1931, was 17 at the time of his crime. In a public letter, Lathrop called the execution of a teenager "a profound miscarriage of justice." She also persuaded three lawyers to help McWilliams appeal his death sentence. Not willing to limit her efforts to this one case, Lathrop organized a nationwide campaign against the execution of minors.

Although Lathrop's national campaign failed, her efforts helped to save McWilliams's life. In April 1933, Henry Horner, the newly elected governor of Illinois, acting on the recommendation of the State Board of Pardons, changed McWilliams's death sentence to 99 years in prison.

Lathrop died on April 15, 1932, the year the Children's Bureau celebrated its 20th anniversary. After Lathrop's death, her friend Jane Addams described the social crusader as "one of the most useful women in the whole country." Of the many tributes to this reformer after her death, perhaps Lathrop's hometown newspaper, the Rockford *Register-Republic*, summed up her life best by saying she had "made a career out of kindness."

As director of the U.S. Women's Bureau, Mary Anderson (1872-1964)—who had come to the United States to earn an independent living for herself—improved the working conditions of thousands of other women.

3

Mary Anderson
Director of the U.S. Women's Bureau

*O*ne day in the early 1950s, an elderly Swedish immigrant named Mary Anderson was discussing her life with a former coworker in the federal government. Anderson, a former domestic servant and factory worker, had become the first director of the U.S. Women's Bureau. Regarding her decision to come to the United States at age 16, Anderson said: "I knew nothing of America, but I thought it was a land of opportunity and that was what I wanted. I have had a wonderful life in America. It has given me everything—friends, work, and a chance to do something in the world." But she was only partly right in saying that the United States had given her everything. Anderson, after all, owed much of her success to herself.

Mary Anderson was born on August 27, 1872, in a small village near the town of Göteborg, on Sweden's southwestern coast. Life was good for Mary, the youngest of Magnus and Matilda Anderson's seven children, even though the Andersons had few luxuries.

Growing up in a small farming community with many friends, Mary enjoyed both the outdoor chores on the family farm and playing games outside with her brothers. She especially loved tending and riding the family's horses. In fact, she might have spent her entire life in Sweden had it not been for the severe agricultural depression that hit that nation during the late 1880s. Because of the economic downturn, the Andersons lost their small farm. This forced Mary to find a way of supporting herself, a difficult task in a small village facing hard times.

Anna, the Andersons' oldest daughter, had moved to the United States in 1887. When she wrote home and suggested that her sisters, Mary and Hilda, join her there, the two young women jumped at the chance. In the spring of 1889, Mary and Hilda Anderson, who spoke no English, joined the immense numbers of immigrants who came to America in the late nineteenth century in search of a better life.

After arriving in Michigan, Mary went to work as a dishwasher, one of the few jobs available in the United

States at that time for someone who had few skills and did not speak English. In 1892, after a series of domestic jobs in Michigan and Wisconsin, Mary moved to Chicago, where Anna and her husband were then living.

In 1894, Anderson got a job as a stitcher at Schwab's, a large Chicago shoe factory. While working there, she had her first contact with the growing trade union movement. The move to this bustling city proved good for Anderson, who liked her new job. Not only was the pay higher and the work more to her liking, but she now had the opportunity to meet new people at work.

In 1899, Anderson and other women workers at Schwab's joined the International Boot and Shoe Workers Union. About a year later, the members in her shop, most of whom were also stitchers, elected Anderson—who by now had learned English—president of the local branch of the union. Anderson also represented her local branch on the union's citywide council and became a delegate to the Chicago Federation of Labor, an organization that coordinated the activities of the city's various trade unions.

In 1905, Anderson joined the Women's Trade Union League (WTUL), which had been formed in 1903 by a group of settlement house workers. The WTUL encouraged working women to participate in trade unions to help them improve their working conditions. The WTUL's membership included both men and women, union members, and people who supported the league's goals but did not belong to a labor union. Anderson's membership in the WTUL changed her life. Through the organization, she formed lifelong friendships, became a union organizer, and eventually joined the federal government.

After joining the WTUL, Anderson continued to hold office in the International Boot and Shoe Workers Union. In 1906, she became a member of its national executive board, and spent more and more of her free time attending the WTUL's meetings and parties at Hull House. There she got to know Jane Addams (the WTUL's first national vice-president), Julia Lathrop, and other residents of the Chicago settlement house.

Anderson also met Margaret Dreier Robins, who would be her close friend for almost 30 years. Robins had been president of the New York chapter of the WTUL until her marriage to Raymond Robins in 1905. In 1907, Robins became WTUL's national president, an office she held until 1922.

In 1910, a group of Chicago garment workers went on strike to protest their long hours of work, low wages, and poor working conditions. The WTUL supported the striking workers, many of whom were women. This strike lasted more than four months and brought the Chicago garment industry to a virtual halt. Because of the efforts of Robins and other members of the WTUL, one business—Hart, Schaffner & Marx—made many concessions to the workers.

Nurses at the Henry Street settlement house helped the poor in New York City, just as reformers at Jane Addams's Hull House had done in Chicago.

Margaret Dreier Robins (1868-1945), who served as president of the Women's Trade Union League for 15 years, believed that women should demand better working conditions, just as men had done.

The contract between Hart, Schaffner & Marx and the garment workers' union was an important breakthrough in labor relations. This firm, which operated Chicago's largest clothing factory, agreed to submit all labor disputes to a committee for arbitration, a process in which an impartial third party recommends a settlement. In addition to providing for arbitration, the contract established minimum hourly wages, limits on the number of hours employers could demand that employees work, and rules for ensuring workers' health and safety.

After the strike ended, Robins asked Anderson to leave her factory job and become a representative for the WTUL. As a union organizer, Anderson's duties were largely educational. She explained to working women how unions operate and how they could help workers obtain better pay and working conditions, and she stressed the necessity of workers acting as a group instead of individually when protesting unfair working conditions. Anderson and the other union leaders knew that strength came with numbers.

At first, Anderson spent much of her time explaining the arbitration process to the Hart, Schaffner & Marx workers. Anderson encouraged them to take their complaints to an arbitrator instead of going on strike—an action she favored only as a last resort. Anderson also worked hard to educate both employers and employees about the need to honor the terms of an agreement. Her experience as a union organizer taught Anderson the importance of working patiently for small improvements, which could add up to significant gains over time.

Anderson continued her work for the International Boot and Shoe Workers Union and the WTUL until the United States entered World War I in April 1917. Shortly afterward, labor leader Samuel Gompers offered her a job. Gompers headed the American Federation of Labor, an umbrella group representing different trade unions. He asked Anderson to join a committee that was trying to persuade U.S. companies to produce military supplies instead of civilian goods. Anderson's subcommittee looked for ways that women could help the war effort by taking industrial jobs—usually held by men—to free men for military service.

Samuel Gompers (1850-1924), who emigrated to the United States from Great Britain in 1863, became a leading figure in the labor movement—fighting for shorter hours, better wages, and more rights for the nation's work force.

While working on this project, Anderson met Mary Van Kleeck, a reformer and social researcher who was studying the possibility of employing women in arsenals, where military weapons were stored. Van Kleeck needed an assistant with experience in trade unions. So early in 1918, she asked Anderson to help her organize a women's division in the army's ordnance department. This division would oversee the employment of women in the army arsenals. Anderson took a three-month leave of absence from her job and moved to Washington, D.C., to join Van Kleeck in the new project.

Anderson had planned to return to Chicago at the end of her three-month stint. But before that time was up, U.S. Secretary of Labor William Wilson asked both Anderson and Van Kleeck to work for the Department of Labor's new agency, which was called Woman in Industry Service. The government had established this wartime agency to monitor the working conditions of women employed in war industries. The two women began work in July 1918, with Van Kleeck as the agency's director and Anderson as her assistant.

Van Kleeck and Anderson frequently found unhealthy and unsafe working conditions in the country's war industries. Moreover, employers often paid women workers less than men with similar job responsibilities. The two women waged a constant battle in support of equal pay for women workers, but they found that employers could easily manipulate wage scales by setting up different job categories for males and females.

Both Van Kleeck and Anderson worked hard to develop standards for women war workers, including limits on the number of hours worked, adequate lunch and rest periods, and a ban on both hazardous work and night work. Although the U.S. government did not approve these standards until December 1918—one month after the war had ended—the standards Van Kleeck and

Anderson developed became the model for future protective rules for working women.

In the summer of 1919, Anderson succeeded Van Kleeck as director of the Woman in Industry Service. (Earlier that year, Congress had approved a one-year extension of the wartime agency's operation.) Meanwhile, the WTUL and other women's organizations pressured Congress to create a permanent government agency to look after the needs of working women.

In June 1920, Congress established the Women's Bureau as part of the Labor Department. Shortly afterward, Democratic president Woodrow Wilson named Anderson the first director of this new agency. Like its

President Woodrow Wilson (1856-1924), who held office from 1913 to 1921, asked the U.S. Senate to support the Nineteenth Amendment, which gave women the right to vote in 1920.

forerunner—the Woman in Industry Service—this new agency was responsible for developing standards and policies to promote the welfare of working women, improve their working conditions, increase their efficiency, and advance their opportunities for profitable work.

After Republican candidate Warren G. Harding won the 1920 presidential election, Mary Anderson—a Democratic political appointee—expected to find herself out of a job. Groups of U.S. women rallied to Anderson's support, however, and Harding reappointed her to head the Women's Bureau. Anderson, who tried not to alienate others, held the office until her retirement in 1944. She served under two Democratic and three Republican presidents.

During the 1920s, many conservatives opposed both labor unions and women's work outside the home. These people insisted that Anderson and other prominent women reformers were part of a group of subversive radicals determined to corrupt American values.

Anderson herself was actually fairly conservative in outlook. She never questioned women's traditional role as mothers and homemakers. While growing up, she fully expected to marry and raise a family one day. She knew from her experience as a union organizer, however, that marriage did not automatically bring women financial security. Even though many employers and male trade unionists claimed that women worked simply for "pin money" to spend on luxuries, Anderson learned that most women worked to support themselves and their families.

Like many other women reformers of her day, Anderson objected to a proposed constitutional amendment guaranteeing equal rights for American women. The Equal Rights Amendment (ERA), first introduced in Congress in 1923, divided women into two hostile camps. Many women, including Anderson, believed that by giving women the *same* rights as men, the ERA would destroy the protective laws Anderson and others had fought so hard to get. Other women, however, believed that the ERA would help women and that the protective laws actually harmed them by keeping women out of better paying jobs.

In the late 1920s, the Women's Bureau, hoping to end the controversy over the ERA, studied the effect of protective laws on working women. The study used most of the bureau's resources and required two years' worth of funds to complete. The in-depth study concluded that the protective laws did not reduce women workers' opportunities. In fact, these laws actually improved working standards for women as well as men. The Women's Bureau study did not persuade the ERA's supporters to drop their fight for the constitutional amendment, however. The unsuccessful push for the ERA continued until the early 1980s.

Democrat Franklin Roosevelt's victory in the 1932 presidential election delighted Anderson. After all, she was a longtime friend of Franklin Roosevelt—whom she had first met when he was an assistant secretary of the navy during World War I—and of his wife, Eleanor. Anderson was especially pleased because she felt that working women could count on the support of First Lady Eleanor Roosevelt, a longtime member of the WTUL.

Anderson was also pleased when President Roosevelt appointed Frances Perkins, a strong supporter of labor reforms, to the position of U.S. secretary of labor in 1933. Perkins became the first woman in U.S. history to be appointed to a president's cabinet. America's working

President Franklin Roosevelt (1882-1945), who held office from 1933 to 1945, appointed several women to federal positions that previously had been filled only by men.

women would have a champion who understood their problems and wanted to fight for their welfare. Anderson, however, grew disappointed because Perkins did not seem particularly interested in the Women's Bureau and did not consult Anderson very often.

During World War II, Anderson struggled with the same problems she had faced during World War I: convincing employers that women could replace men in most jobs—thus freeing the men for military service—and making sure that women workers received the same pay as men for the same work. Anderson had some success in these efforts, but she was growing tired and discouraged. In June 1944, when she was 71, she retired from government service.

In 1962, on Anderson's 90th birthday, Secretary of Labor Arthur Goldberg gave her the Labor Department's Award of Merit in recognition of her many contributions to the welfare of working women during her 25 years as director of the Women's Bureau. Anderson died at her Washington, D.C., home on January 29, 1964.

Mary Anderson, pictured here at a political reception during the 1950s, dedicated her life to improving the working conditions and increasing the wages of women employed outside the home.

Frances Perkins (1880-1965), the first woman ever appointed to a president's cabinet, overcame many obstacles during her 12 years as U.S. secretary of labor.

4

Frances Perkins
Secretary of Labor

Shortly after Franklin Roosevelt won the 1932 presidential election, First Lady Eleanor Roosevelt began to encourage her husband to appoint women to high-level offices in the federal government. One such appointment went to Frances Perkins, who had worked for Roosevelt while he was governor of New York. In 1933, the president named Perkins the U.S. secretary of labor, making her the first woman to serve in a presidential cabinet.

Although she once said, "I hate politics," First Lady Eleanor Roosevelt (1884-1962) was a member of several political organizations, and she often spoke and traveled on behalf of her husband, President Franklin D. Roosevelt.

Fannie Coralie Perkins, the first of Fred and Susan Perkins's two children, was born in Boston on April 10, 1880. When Fannie was two, her parents moved to Worcester, Massachusetts. After graduating from the Worcester Classical High School, Fannie attended Mount Holyoke College, a women's college in South Hadley, Massachusetts, about 40 miles west of Worcester. Although most women were not encouraged to study science at that time, Fannie Perkins graduated in 1902 with a degree in chemistry.

Perkins then spent two years teaching school in Worcester before accepting a teaching job at a girls' school in Lake Forest, Illinois, a suburb of Chicago. Around that time, Perkins began calling herself *Frances* instead of Fannie. To make herself seem younger, she began telling others she was born in 1882—two years after her actual date of birth. Little did Frances Perkins know that lying about the year of her birth would cause her serious problems later in life.

While working in Lake Forest, Perkins spent much of her free time volunteering at the Hull House and other Chicago settlement houses. There, she had her first dealings with labor unions, observed how employers sometimes cheated their employees out of their wages, and saw the need for social reform. As a result of her experience in Illinois, Perkins decided to become a social worker.

Moving to Philadelphia in 1908, Perkins did social work while taking graduate courses in economics and sociology at the University of Pennsylvania. In the summer of 1909, she went to New York City for additional studies at Columbia University, where she earned a master's degree in 1910. After graduation, she also worked as secretary of the New York City Consumers' League, a reform organization that advocated better working conditions for U.S. workers and an end to child labor.

The work Perkins did for the league involved periodic visits to Albany, New York, to persuade members of the state legislature to vote for laws that the league supported. While engaging in these lobbying efforts, Perkins met three state lawmakers who would help shape her later career—Franklin Roosevelt, Robert Wagner, and Alfred Smith.

In 1912, Perkins resigned from her job with the Consumers' League and accepted a position with a citizens' lobbying group, the Committee on Public Safety of the City of New York. She again worked with Wagner and Smith, who were members of the New York State Factory Investigating Commission. The state legislature had created this commission in 1911 to examine working conditions in the state's manufacturing industries.

As she had done while working for the Consumers' League, Perkins visited factories and other work sites to see for herself what was happening. The combined efforts of the Committee on Public Safety and the Factory Investigating Commission resulted in the enactment of several state laws that improved conditions for the state's workers. In 1915, after these laws went into effect, the state legislature disbanded the Factory Investigating Commission, believing that the commission was no longer needed.

By that time, Perkins had married Paul Wilson, a New York City economist. The wedding took place on September 26, 1913, at Grace Church in New York. Wilson was 37, and Perkins was 33. After the wedding, Perkins continued to work for the Committee on Public

Safety. However, she had to stop working for several months in 1915. That spring, she gave birth to a child, who died shortly afterward. In December 1916, Perkins had a second child, Susanna. Because Perkins and her husband worked outside the home, she hired a nurse to help care for their daughter.

After Susanna's birth, Perkins continued to do volunteer work for various groups. Some of her most successful projects were with the Maternity Center Association, which worked to reduce infant and maternal mortality. Because of her own experience with the birth and death of a child, Perkins had a personal commitment to this endeavor.

In 1919, shortly after his election as governor of New York, Al Smith gave Perkins a job as a member of the New York State Industrial Commission, which oversaw working conditions in the state's manufacturing industries. Perkins, the first woman to serve on the commission, was also one of the highest paid women in the state government. An annual salary of $8,000 was a substantial sum at a time when the average American earned about $1,240 per year.

Because her husband was suffering his first bout with a mental disorder that would trouble him for the rest of his life, Perkins needed the money. Paul Wilson's unpredictable waves of depression and excitement eventually led to periods of confinement in a private mental hospital, making Perkins the family breadwinner.

When Smith lost his bid for reelection as governor of New York in 1920, Perkins also lost her appointment to the New York State Industrial Commission. In 1922, however, she was reappointed when Smith was again elected governor. This time, he held office until 1928, when he made a losing run for the presidency. In 1926, Perkins moved from being simply a member of the New York State Industrial Commission to being its chair. Perkins held this office until Franklin Roosevelt replaced Smith as governor of New York after the 1928 election.

Because Roosevelt, like Smith, was a Democrat, Perkins expected the new governor to reappoint her as head of the Industrial Commission. To her surprise,

Al Smith (1873-1944) ran for president on the Democratic ticket in 1928 but lost the election to Republican Herbert Hoover.

Roosevelt offered her instead the job of industrial commissioner for the state of New York. At first, she was unsure about taking the job because, although the pay was higher than her previous work for the state, the position involved many new responsibilities and longer hours.

Perkins had worked only part time on the industrial board. If she accepted Roosevelt's proposed job, however, she would be working full time and would be supervising the day-to-day operation of the state labor department and its 1,800 employees. Despite her initial reluctance, Perkins accepted the appointment. By that time, her husband, who had worked off and on for several years, had stopped working altogether. Perkins could not afford to turn down the extra money she would earn as industrial commissioner.

In 1932, Franklin Roosevelt won his bid for the presidency of the United States. When the newly elected president asked Perkins to join his administration as the U.S. secretary of labor, she hesitated. The Children's Bureau and the Women's Bureau, both part of the Department of Labor, interested Perkins. Additionally, Perkins's experience in New York made her qualified for this important job. But Perkins was unsure whether to accept this new position. The three previous secretaries of labor—all men—had been labor union officials before serving in the cabinet office, and Perkins had neither worked in a factory nor joined a labor union.

Perkins was also concerned about how her move to Washington, D.C., would affect her husband, who was then a patient in a private mental hospital in a New York City suburb. After Roosevelt sweetened his offer by assuring her that as president he would push for several of the labor reforms Perkins had supported in New York, she accepted the cabinet post.

When Perkins took office in March 1933, the United States was in a deep economic depression. As Perkins later said, "Economically the country was on the ragged edge of nothing." She wanted to begin work immediately on labor reforms, but some chores badly needed her attention: First, she had to exterminate a nest of cockroaches in her desk! More importantly, she had to rid the Bureau of Immigration (then part of the Labor Department) of the racketeers who dominated its work force.

Handling the many labor disputes that flared up in the 1930s gave Perkins more trouble. Despite the high rate of unemployment during this period, many workers risked their jobs by going on strike to improve their working conditions. Some of these strikes resulted in violence. Many people wondered whether a woman would be tough enough to stand up to the polished corporate executives and the hard-boiled union bosses.

Perkins proved to be both tough and fair. She always insisted that employers bargain in good faith with the unions, but she expected the unions to live up to their part of a bargain, too. Her hard work behind the scenes contributed to the peaceful settlement of many labor disputes, and she eventually earned the grudging respect of most union leaders.

During President Roosevelt's first two terms in office, Perkins developed several plans to bring the United States out of the Great Depression and to relieve the misery of the high percentage of Americans who suffered from very low wages, poor working conditions, or unemployment. Robert Wagner, a member of the U.S. Senate and a friend from Perkins's days as a lobbyist, supported many of these reforms. The reforms included a public works program to provide jobs for the unemployed, tight controls on child labor, and legislation regulating hours of work and establishing minimum wages.

Perkins was largely responsible for the development of the Social Security Act, one of the most enduring reforms of the 1930s. In 1934, President Roosevelt asked Perkins to head the Committee on Economic Security, which drafted this landmark law. The Social Security Act, which Congress passed in 1935 and the U.S. Supreme Court upheld two years later, included both unemployment and retirement insurance. Perkins had advocated these reforms while she was a New York state official.

Despite Perkins's solid accomplishments as secretary of labor, many people criticized her. Some people made jokes about her dowdy dresses and the small black

Frances Perkins and other public officials
watch as President Franklin Roosevelt signs
the Social Security Act into law in 1935.

hat she almost always wore in public. One critic said the
hat "looked like someone sat on it," and journalists often
referred to her as "Ma Perkins" (the title of a popular
daytime radio show) or the "old maid secretary of labor."

Likewise, many reporters considered Perkins
unfriendly, snobbish, and impersonal when she brushed
them off with dry statistics about her work as secretary of
labor instead of speaking more freely about her personal
life. Although the White House press corps knew that
Perkins's husband had emotional problems, they did not

ask her directly about him. Doing so would have been considered highly disrespectful at that time.

In fact, although Perkins was a public official, few people other than her friends and associates even knew she was married. Society had learned more about mental illness since the days when reformers Dorothea Dix and Julia Lathrop had crusaded for more humane treatment of the mentally ill. But many people—perhaps even Perkins herself—still thought mental illness was somehow shameful and should not be discussed openly.

Moreover, the decisions that Perkins had made to change her first name and lie about the year of her birth caused trouble for her after she became Roosevelt's secretary of labor. The president's political enemies were trying to find ways to discredit him and the members of his administration. When they investigated Frances Perkins (who said that she had been born in 1882), they found no public record of the birth. Frances Perkins was obviously hiding something, they concluded.

After further investigation, the president's political enemies uncovered a record of a marriage in Newton, Massachusetts, in 1910 between a man named Paul Wilson (the same name as Perkins's husband) and a woman named Matilda Watski. They then claimed that Frances Perkins was really Matilda Watski and that she was a Russian Jew and a Communist. They argued that she was not fit to serve in the cabinet. (Anti-Semitism and fear of communism were widespread at that time.)

Like many public officials throughout history, Frances Perkins—who was criticized for everything from her heritage to her choice in hats—learned that rumors and speculation can damage a political career.

Perkins wrote a public letter giving the correct date and place of her marriage, but the rumors regarding her background persisted. She never convinced everyone that she was not really Matilda Watski.

The whispering campaign against Perkins reached a climax in 1939. At that time, J. Parnell Thomas, a conservative Republican congressman from New Jersey, introduced a resolution asking the House of Representatives to impeach Perkins from office because she failed to enforce the country's immigration laws. Thomas said that Perkins had refused to expel Harry Bridges from the United States for taking part in a communist conspiracy against the government. Some of

Perkins's opponents had already spread rumors that she protected the Australian-born labor leader because he was one of her relatives. But Perkins and Bridges were not related.

Actually, the Bureau of Immigration, which Perkins oversaw, had begun action to expel Bridges after several people claimed that they had seen him participating in Communist Party activities. Perkins had stopped the proceedings against Bridges on the advice of the U.S. Department of Justice. The Justice Department wanted her to wait for the outcome of the court action in a similar case before proceeding further against Bridges. Even

New Jersey congressman J. Parnell Thomas thought Frances Perkins was not qualified to run the Department of Labor—and tried to convince others to agree with him.

though she was on solid legal ground in delaying the expulsion of Bridges, Perkins voluntarily testified before the congressional committee investigation on the Thomas resolution. After her testimony, the U.S. House of Representatives voted to take no further action on the resolution.

Perkins, who was secretary of labor throughout Roosevelt's 12 years as president, served briefly under President Harry Truman before resigning in 1945. In September 1946, Truman appointed her to the Civil Service Commission, which had overall supervision of the federal work force. Perkins held this position until 1953, one year after her husband's death.

After her retirement from the federal government, Perkins traveled around the country lecturing on college campuses and elsewhere. In 1957, she became a visiting professor at Cornell University, in Ithaca, New York. She held this title until her death on May 14, 1965.

In 1963, Perkins returned to Washington, D. C., to celebrate the 30th anniversary of Franklin Roosevelt's inauguration as president and the 50th anniversary of the establishment of the Department of Labor. During the Labor Department's anniversary dinner, President John F. Kennedy praised Perkins, whom he called "the grand old lady of the labor movement." The young president smiled as he added in reference to her accomplishments as labor secretary: "They were controversial and Madam Perkins, who looked so quiet and peaceful and sweet, was

Frances Perkins (far right) was the guest speaker at a 1958 Democratic Women's Luncheon.

also one of the most controversial, dangerous figures that roamed the United States in the 1930s," he said.

In 1979, Congress named the new Washington, D.C., headquarters of the Labor Department in honor of Perkins. (This was the first time a federal government building bore a woman's name.) In 1980, the U.S. Postal Service issued a stamp bearing an image of Perkins wearing the small black hat that had become her trademark during her years as a cabinet officer.

Ruth Bryan Owen Rohde (1885-1954), whose
interest in politics dated back to her childhood, had
a distinguished career in the U.S. Congress before
representing her country overseas.

5

Ruth Bryan Owen Rohde
Congresswoman Turned Diplomat

*R*uth Bryan was born into the world of politics. Her grandfather, Silas Bryan, was a judge in southern Illinois who served two terms in the state senate during the 1850s and ran a losing campaign for the U.S. House of Representatives in 1872. Ruth's father, William Jennings Bryan, served two terms in the House of Representatives in the 1890s as a U.S. representative from Nebraska. He later ran for president of the United States three times, but he lost each race. Bryan, like his father before him, was a Democrat at a time when the Republicans dominated U.S. politics.

Ruth Bryan, the first of William and Mary Baird Bryan's three children, was born on October 2, 1885, in Jacksonville, Illinois. When Ruth was almost two, the Bryans moved to Lincoln, Nebraska, where her father practiced law with a former classmate from law school. After moving to Nebraska, Mary Bryan completed the law studies she had begun in Illinois, but she never practiced law.

Politically ambitious, William Bryan knew that joining the Republican Party was the surest road to political success in Nebraska. (In the late nineteenth century, Nebraska was a solidly Republican state.) However, Bryan, a staunch Democrat, refused to abandon his political party. Instead, he tried to make as many friends as possible in his new home by becoming active in civic and political clubs.

William Bryan's genial manner made him popular in the political circles of Lincoln, Nebraska. He made friends in other parts of the state too. Traveling by train, on horseback, in a buggy, or on a farm wagon, Bryan attracted large crowds wherever he spoke. His tactics paid off in 1890, when the voters of Nebraska's First Congressional District elected him to the U.S. House of Representatives.

Ruth Bryan's political education began at home in Lincoln during her father's election campaign. This

*Nebraska
representative
William
Jennings Bryan
(1860-1925)
became a
political role
model to his
daughter.*

education continued after the family moved to
Washington, D.C. There, six-year-old Ruth got a firsthand look at congressional politics. She often sat with her
mother in the House visitors' gallery, peering down at
the members as they debated or voted on proposed laws.
Sometimes she even sat beside her father in the House
chamber while he made a speech. As an adult, Ruth
would use the political skills she had learned by watching
her father.

   In 1896, 11-year-old Ruth had a chance to see
another aspect of American politics. That year, her father
ran for president. (Both the Democrats and the new

People's—or Populist—Party had chosen him as their candidate.) Bryan often brought his family along as he toured the country by train, speaking to the assembled crowds at local railroad stations and other places. But Bryan did not win enough votes to become president in the 1896 election. In 1900, William Bryan ran for president a second time, but he again lost.

Ruth, an intelligent student, entered college the following year. By the time her father made his third and last try for the presidency in 1908, Ruth, who served as his campaign secretary, was trying to end an unhappy marriage. She had dropped out of the University of Nebraska in 1903 to marry a young artist named William Leavitt. The couple had two children before divorcing in 1909.

Ruth did not remain single very long. In 1910, she married Reginald Owen, an officer in the British Royal Engineers. The Owens lived in Jamaica until 1913. That year, they moved to England, where their son, Reginald Jr., was born. After the outbreak of World War I in 1914, Ruth Owen worked on war relief projects while studying nursing. In 1915, she took two-year-old Reginald to Cairo, Egypt, where she worked as a nurse in a military hospital.

After the war ended in 1918, the Owen family moved to Florida, where Ruth's parents were living. Her fourth child, Helen Rudd Owen, was born there in 1920. By then, Major Owen had developed a disabling kidney

Before entering politics, Ruth Bryan Owen worked as a nurse for a military hospital in Cairo, Egypt, during the First World War.

disease. To supplement her husband's military pension, Ruth Owen spent part of each year traveling around the country giving lectures, as her father had done for many years. Her eloquent speaking ability and her father's fame made her a popular speaker. Like her father, Ruth Owen was concerned with community affairs, and she was active in a number of civic, religious, and educational organizations in the Miami area.

In 1926, one year after her father's death, Ruth Owen decided to try her hand at electoral politics. So she ran for the Democratic nomination for the U.S. House of Representatives in Florida's Fourth Congressional District, which stretched along Florida's eastern coastline from Jacksonville to Key West.

At that time, many Florida voters were not ready to elect a woman to represent them in Congress, even though the Nineteenth Amendment granting women the right to vote had been part of the U.S. Constitution for six years. Nevertheless, Ruth Owen ran a strong race in the Democratic primary, losing by fewer than 800 votes.

Two years later, after the death of her husband, Ruth Owen again ran for the U.S. Congress. Using some of the same tactics that had helped her father win a House seat almost half a century earlier, she succeeded in winning the election. She toured Florida's fourth district for months before the actual election. In speech after speech, Owen explained what she would do for the state as a member of Congress.

Since the mid-1800s, women had fought to gain more political power. But many people in the 1920s were still uncomfortable with the idea of women in government.

Of course, Owen's transportation was more modern than her father's had been back in 1896. Instead of traveling by train or buggy, Owen campaigned in a green automobile, which she named "The Spirit of Florida." The voters of her district gave Owen a 30,000-vote majority over her opponent in the 1928 election, making her one of the first women in the southern United States to win a seat in the U.S. Congress.

Owen's election victory did not guarantee her a House seat, however. Her defeated opponent challenged her election on the grounds that because she had married a British subject in 1910, she had not been a U.S. citizen long enough to qualify for House membership. (The Constitution specifies that a member of the House must have been a citizen for at least seven years.)

Throughout much of U.S. history, a woman's citizenship depended on that of her husband. A 1907 law stated that a woman who married an *alien* (someone who was not an American citizen) automatically lost her U.S. citizenship. In 1922, however, Congress passed the Cable Act, which made the citizenship status of married women independent of their husbands' status. But the Cable Act allowed women who had lost their citizenship by marrying aliens to become U.S. citizens again only if they declared their intent to resume their citizenship.

Resuming citizenship by declaring intent was difficult because a woman could make the required declaration only by appearing in a federal court on the date when an immigration official was there to accept it. Because of her lecturing schedule, Owen was unable to satisfy the requirements of the Cable Act until 1925, when she became a U.S. citizen again. Thus, according to her defeated opponent, Owen had been a U.S. citizen for only three years—not the necessary seven—at the time of the 1928 election.

Refusing to accept defeat, Owen appeared before the House Committee on Elections and defended her right to a seat in Congress. In her defense, she condemned the laws that gave women fewer rights than men. Pointing out that no American man had ever lost his citizenship by marrying an alien, Owen argued that she had lost her citizenship in 1910 because she was a woman, not simply because of her marital status. Impressed by her argument, the U.S. House voted to allow Owen to occupy the contested seat. (Congress later made the rules regarding citizenship identical for men and women.)

After taking her House seat, Owen requested and received an appointment to the House Foreign Affairs Committee. Despite her interest in foreign policy, Owen also remained attentive to domestic affairs. She persuaded Congress to authorize money to fight an infestation of Mediterranean fruit flies in Florida's citrus trees and introduced a bill that later resulted in the creation of Everglades National Park in southern Florida.

No one ran against Owen in the 1930 election. By 1932, however, many Americans were clamoring for the repeal of the controversial Eighteenth Amendment, which had started the era of Prohibition. This amendment, which had become law in January 1920, forbade people from manufacturing or selling alcoholic beverages. In adopting this amendment, lawmakers had hoped to eliminate the social problems caused by excessive drinking.

By the early 1930s, however, many Americans concluded that Prohibition had failed. After all, the illegal liquor trade was booming, and gunfights between rival bootleggers often erupted on city streets. Also, police raids on illegal drinking places—called *speakeasies*—often netted honest citizens who were merely guilty of drinking beer.

Although Owen supported Prohibition, she was not a staunch Prohibitionist. Instead, she favored allowing the nation's voters to decide whether to keep the law. In spite of Owen's middle-ground stand on this issue, Florida residents voted her out of Congress in the 1932 election. Many voters had associated Owen with her father, who publicly opposed alcohol consumption.

Ruth Owen accepted defeat with grace. Before her term was up, she voted to repeal the Eighteenth Amendment, an action she knew the voters of her district would support. The repeal became effective in December 1933, after the legislatures of 36 states voted in favor of it.

Saloons filled up quickly when Prohibition was repealed in 1933 and alcohol became legal for the first time in 13 years.

Owen's 1932 defeat kept her out of the public eye for only a short time. In March 1933, President Franklin Roosevelt named her U.S. ambassador to Denmark. The appointment was another "first" for Owen, as she became the first American woman to head a diplomatic mission to a foreign country. Her official title was "envoy extraordinary and minister plenipotentiary."

The American press generally favored Owen's appointment. Her wit, charm, and political skills had made her one of the most well-liked politicians in the nation. In addition, her experience as a member of the

Close friends Ruth Bryan Owen (right) and First Lady Eleanor Roosevelt walk down the south steps of the White House.

House Foreign Affairs Committee was a decided asset for the newly appointed diplomat.

The citizens of Denmark liked Owen too. One newspaper in Copenhagen commented approvingly on Owen's arrival in the Danish capital by remarking that instead of a diplomat with "striped trousers, with a monocle and a hard-set mouth, . . . President Roosevelt's new lady-minister disembarked . . . smiling and laughing, with arms full of roses, small Danish and American flags and a beautiful grandchild with yellow curls."

The Danes' affection for Owen was not one-sided. During her previous visits to this small European country, Owen had acquired a genuine love for Denmark and its people. Before long, she fell in love with Borge Rohde, a captain in the Danish Royal Guards. The couple was married in 1936 in a ceremony at the Roosevelts' home in Hyde Park, New York. Ruth Bryan Owen Rohde expected to continue as U.S. minister to Denmark after her marriage, but she soon found this to be impossible.

Once again, Ruth Rohde's citizenship was the problem. By marrying a Dane, she automatically became a citizen of Denmark. Although she had not given up her American citizenship, her dual status made the task of representing the United States in Denmark difficult. Because of this, Rohde resigned her post, and she and her new husband moved to the United States.

Rohde spent the next few years lecturing, writing, and serving on various civic and political boards. In 1945,

Rohde became a special assistant to the U.S. State Department and helped to draft the charter of the United Nations. In 1949, President Harry Truman named Rohde an alternate delegate to the United Nations General Assembly. She also headed the executive committee of the United Nations Speakers' Research Committee from 1948 until her death in 1954.

Members of the U.N. General Assembly held their first meeting in January 1946 and continue to meet in the United Nations building in New York to work toward achieving international peace.

While in Denmark to accept an award from King Frederick IX for her contributions to Danish-American friendship, she died of a heart attack on July 26, 1954. Her family buried her ashes in Copenhagen, the Danish city she had grown to love.

As a member of a political family, Ruth Bryan Owen Rohde grew up assuming that politics would be part of her life. She never accepted the idea that politics was a job for men only. Moreover, like her father, she was always ready to bounce back from defeat and try again.

Although her career as a diplomat lasted only a short time, Rohde believed that a diplomatic career was one for which women were well suited. In her view, when it came to "enthusiasm for those things which make for peace rather than war—woman is on her own sure ground." Her father, a firm believer in women's rights and peace among nations, would have applauded this statement.

Florence Ellinwood Allen (1884-1965), the first woman to serve on the U.S. appeals court, fought to give other women more opportunities in government.

6

Florence Ellinwood Allen
Court of Appeals Judge

*O*n March 23, 1934, Florence Ellinwood Allen received an unusual gift for her 50th birthday. On that day, she was appointed a judge on the U.S. Court of Appeals—the highest judicial rank any American woman had ever held in the federal government. The appointment was the latest in a series of "firsts" for this Ohio lawyer. Allen had previously been the first woman to serve as an assistant prosecutor in Ohio, the first woman judge in an Ohio trial court, and the first woman in the country to serve as a judge on a state's highest court.

Florence Ellinwood Allen, the third daughter of Clarence and Corinne Tuckerman Allen's seven children, was born on March 23, 1884, in Salt Lake City, Utah. One of Corinne Allen's ancestors came to the United States on the *Mayflower*, and one of Clarence Allen's ancestors fought in the American Revolution. Both of her parents were well educated and interested in public affairs.

After moving to Utah, Clarence Allen, a graduate of the Western Reserve University in Cleveland, Ohio, studied law and later served three terms in the territorial legislature. After Utah became a state in 1896, he also served one term in the U.S. House of Representatives. Corinne Allen had attended Smith College in Northampton, Massachusetts, for two years before her marriage. She helped to establish a public library in Salt Lake City and was active in several women's organizations in Utah.

The Allen children, like those in most families, had to help with the household chores. Young Florence chopped wood, filled the wood box that supplied the family's cooking and heating needs, and tended the yard. Her outdoor work gave the tall youngster a love for vigorous exercise that stayed with her for the rest of her life. She especially enjoyed hiking and mountain climbing, a hobby that grew out of her childhood walks through the foothills of the Wasatch Mountains near Salt Lake City.

A bright child, Florence learned the Greek alphabet by age four and began to study Latin at age seven.

Florence entered Salt Lake College in 1897 at age 13. (Despite its name, the school was actually a high school that offered college-preparatory courses.)

During her two years at Salt Lake College, Florence studied music and became a skilled debater. Her forceful speaking voice and logical arguments led her father to comment that if she had been a boy, he would have suggested a career as a lawyer. A career practicing law, however, was far from young Florence's mind. After all, most professions—including law—were generally closed to women in the late nineteenth century. Moreover, her musical talent made a career as a concert pianist seem possible.

In 1900, 16-year-old Florence joined one of her older sisters as a student at the Women's College of Western Reserve University, her father's alma mater. An enthusiastic participant in college activities, she was president of her freshman class, editor of the college literary magazine, and frequently appeared in college theater performances. Her height and deep speaking voice sometimes earned her a "male" leading role in the college plays.

After receiving a bachelor's degree with honors from Western Reserve in 1904, Florence Allen worked as a teacher and music critic. She knew by then that her musical abilities were not great enough for her to earn a living as a concert pianist. Still, she remained unsure about spending the rest of her life as a teacher or music critic.

To help resolve her uncertainty, Allen enrolled in a graduate program at Western Reserve and in 1908 received a master's degree in political science. During her graduate studies, Allen decided that her father's half-joking suggestion about a law career made sense. She would become a lawyer.

Allen wanted to study law at Western Reserve, but because that university did not admit women to its professional schools, she enrolled in the University of Chicago's law school instead. Allen was one of a handful of women students enrolled there, and she did very well academically. By the end of the school year, she ranked second in her class.

In 1910, Allen accepted a job as a social worker in New York. She intended to continue her law studies in evening classes at one of the city's law schools. Since her first choice, the Columbia University law school, refused to admit women, she enrolled in New York University's law school. In 1913, she received her law degree.

While in New York, Allen became involved in the campaign to give women the right to vote. In 1911, Maud Wood Park, executive director of the National College Women's Equal Suffrage League, had hired Allen as her assistant secretary. Allen's duties put her in touch with many of the leaders of the women's suffrage movement. These contacts would later prove valuable to Allen during her career as a lawyer and judge.

After meeting the requirements to practice law in Ohio in 1914, Allen continued her work for women's suffrage. In 1915, she went to Massachusetts to help with that state's drive for voting rights for women. The following year, she was a delegate to the national convention of the National American Woman Suffrage Association. Additionally, Allen successfully represented the Cleveland

During a 1917 New York City parade, women's suffrage supporters march to help gain support for their cause.

Woman Suffrage Party in a lawsuit involving women's right to vote in municipal elections in some Ohio cities.

Florence Allen also became active in Democratic politics in Ohio. Three years after campaigning for Woodrow Wilson's reelection as president in 1916, she became a Democratic National Committee representative for Ohio. Her political connections resulted in a job offer in 1919 to become the assistant prosecuting attorney for Cuyahoga County, where Cleveland is located.

Allen accepted the offer and became the first woman in the United States to work as a public prosecutor. The work was very demanding; Allen often received the file on a case involving a minor crime only moments before the trial began. Her job, however, provided good experience, for it gave her a thorough grounding in the operation of a trial court.

She put her training to use on the other side of the judge's bench. In August 1920—immediately after the adoption of the Nineteenth Amendment, which gave women the right to vote—Allen announced her intention to run for election as a judge in the Cuyahoga County Court of Common Pleas. (This was the same court in which she had prosecuted criminal cases.)

By the time Allen made her announcement, the political parties had already picked their candidates for that year's election. Therefore, in order to run in the general election, Allen had to get 2,000 voters to sign a petition asking that her name be put on the ballot. Busy with her duties as assistant prosecutor, Allen delegated the job of getting signatures to the women who had been active in the women's suffrage drive.

These women did a superb job and obtained enough signatures within a few days. Allen, who had the support of women in both the Democratic and Republican parties, swept to victory in the 1920 general election. She received more votes than any of the nine male candidates for the county judgeship.

When Allen took office, the judges on the Cuyahoga County Court wanted her to preside over a new court that would handle only divorce cases. She resisted this attempt to keep her from the full range of cases. Allen argued that, as an unmarried woman, she was no more qualified than the male judges (most of whom were married) to handle divorce cases. Winning the argument, Allen soon began judging both civil and criminal cases.

As a trial judge, Allen was tough but fair. She did not hesitate to impose a death sentence on a gangster who had killed two men during a robbery, even though she had received death threats during his trial. She also imposed a prison term on a city court judge found guilty of lying under oath. In her sentencing, she pointed out that judges, like ordinary citizens, must obey the law.

In 1922, Allen ran for a seat on the Ohio Supreme Court, an office that required her to campaign throughout the state. As in 1920, she obtained a place on the ballot by petitioning instead of running in a political party primary. Once again, the state's women supported her, forming "Florence Allen clubs" throughout Ohio to help with the petition drive and the general election campaign.

Allen herself toured the state in her automobile, which she named "Gypsy." She scored an easy victory in the 1922 election, winning by 50,000 votes and becoming the first woman to win a seat on Ohio's highest court. In 1928, Allen won reelection to the Ohio Supreme Court by an even larger number of votes than she had in the 1922 election.

During her two terms as a state supreme court judge, Allen made two unsuccessful attempts to win a legislative office. In 1926, she ran a losing campaign for the Democratic nomination for the U.S. Senate. In 1932, she ran for the U.S. House of Representatives against a popular Republican congressman in a heavily Republican district. The Democrats swept most national offices that year, but Allen lost her bid for a House seat by a small margin.

After her 1932 defeat, Allen had little enthusiasm for running for a third term on the Ohio Supreme Court. So when Judge Smith Hickenlooper's death in December 1933 created a vacancy on the U.S. Court of Appeals for the Sixth Circuit, Allen decided to go after the job. If she managed to obtain the position, she would be the Court of Appeals judge who would oversee Kentucky, Tennessee, Michigan, and Ohio.

Florence Ellinwood Allen (far left) and other Democratic officials listen as James Farley, chairman of the Democratic National Committee, predicts that Franklin Roosevelt will win by 10 million votes in the 1932 presidential election.

Instead, Franklin Roosevelt received nearly 23 million votes in the election, defeating Republican incumbent Herbert Hoover by more than 7 million votes.

Even though no woman had ever served on a federal appeals court, Allen had an excellent chance for the appointment because newly elected President Franklin Roosevelt had already appointed several women to federal offices. Besides, Allen had many supporters both within and outside government circles.

Eager to see her receive this appointment, Allen's friends from her women's suffrage days—Democrats and Republicans—campaigned for her. First Lady Eleanor Roosevelt and Molly Dewson, who headed the Women's Division of the Democratic National Committee, added

Molly Dewson (1874-1962), director of the Women's Division of the Democratic National Committee from 1933 to 1936, spent her career encouraging women to become more active in politics.

their support. Their work paid off when President Roosevelt nominated Allen to fill the appeals court vacancy in March 1934. Later in the month, the Senate unanimously confirmed Allen's nomination, clearing the way for this special 50th birthday present.

As an appeals court judge, Allen had a voice in deciding a wide range of issues concerning federal law. One of her most important decisions involved the constitutionality of the Tennessee Valley Authority Act, which Congress had passed in 1933. The law authorized a federal agency—the Tennessee Valley Authority (TVA)—to

Though she was unsuccessful when running for Congress, Florence Ellinwood Allen had no trouble convincing the U.S. Senate to confirm her nomination as a U.S. Court of Appeals judge.

The Tennessee Valley Authority, which Congress established in 1933, was controversial because many people did not think the federal government should be involved in providing electricity and other resources traditionally provided by private companies.

build dams to control flooding and improve navigation on the Tennessee River. (This waterway flows through several southern states before emptying into the Ohio River.) To recover part of its cost, the TVA would then sell the electric power that resulted from the operation of the dams.

In 1937, Judge Allen presided over hearings on a lawsuit that several electric utility companies had filed against the TVA. The lawyers for the utilities argued that the real purpose of the Tennessee Valley Authority Act was to compete unfairly with them in the production and sale of electric power. They insisted that the enterprise exceeded the constitutional authority of the federal government.

The case, which involved many technical issues, promised to drag on for a long time. Judge Allen, however, devised several shortcuts to speed the hearings. In January 1938, she upheld the constitutionality of the law and noted that the power of Congress to regulate interstate commerce gave it sufficient authority to construct the dams and sell the resulting electric power. The U.S. Supreme Court upheld her decision in 1939.

The court on which Allen served was just one step lower than the Supreme Court. Therefore, when vacancies on the U.S. Supreme Court occurred during President Roosevelt's second term, both Eleanor Roosevelt and Molly Dewson tried to persuade the president to add another "first" to Allen's list by nominating her as a Supreme Court justice. The president did not follow their suggestion, however. During his presidency, Roosevelt named nine Supreme Court justices. All of them were men.

Despite the continued efforts of women's groups on her behalf, Allen fared no better under presidents Harry Truman and Dwight Eisenhower. Truman's four Supreme Court nominees and Eisenhower's five nominees were also all men. Eisenhower's last appointment in 1958 (the year before Allen's retirement) went to Judge Potter Stewart, Allen's colleague on the appeals court.

When Allen died on September 12, 1966, the Supreme Court still did not include a woman justice. In 1954, Eleanor Roosevelt had predicted that despite the many obstacles women lawyers faced, a woman would someday sit on the U.S. Supreme Court. She added that

As late as 1966, the year Florence Ellinwood Allen died, there were still no women or minorities on the Supreme Court. The 1966 Court (from left to right): justices Tom C. Clark, Byron White, Hugo Black, William J. Brennan, Earl Warren (chief justice), Potter Stewart, William O. Douglas, Abe Fortas, and John M. Harlan.

In 1981, Sandra Day O'Connor— who had served as an Arizona state senator and a judge on the Arizona Court of Appeals— became the first woman appointed to the Supreme Court.

when that day came, the new justice "might make a little bow to Florence Allen, who by her own distinguished career helped to make it possible."

Justice Sandra Day O'Connor, the first woman appointed to the Supreme Court, and Ruth Bader Ginsburg, who became the second woman on the high court in 1993, probably never took Eleanor Roosevelt's suggestion literally. However, both must certainly recognize how much Florence Allen did to smooth the way for them and for countless other women who have since decided to make the administration of justice their life's work.

Constance Baker Motley, the first African-American woman to serve as a federal judge, devoted her career to ending racial discrimination.

7

Constance Baker Motley
Civil Rights Lawyer and Judge

*W*hen 22-year-old Constance Baker entered law school at Columbia University in 1944, a successful career as a lawyer seemed unlikely, and an appointment as a federal judge seemed almost impossible. Like Florence Ellinwood Allen, who was then a judge on the U.S. Court of Appeals for the Sixth Circuit, Constance Baker would need considerable intelligence, strong determination, and a little luck to achieve success in the field of law. Allen had succeeded in spite of one serious obstacle in her path: She was female in a society that often discriminated against women. Baker had an additional obstacle, however: She was a black woman in a society that also discriminated against minorities.

Constance Baker, the daughter of Willoughby and Rachel Huggins Baker (both immigrants from the British West Indies) was born in New Haven, Connecticut, on September 14, 1921. The family lived near Yale University, where Willoughby Baker worked as a cook.

While growing up, young Constance had little reason to believe that she would be able to attend college one day. The Bakers could not afford college tuition for the members of their large family, and they thought a college education was impractical for a young woman—especially a young black woman. During Constance's childhood, most black women in New Haven worked either as domestic servants or as part of office cleaning crews.

In 1938, when Constance was a junior in high school, the U.S. Supreme Court handed down a decision that represented a significant breakthrough on the issue of equal rights for black Americans. The case involved Lloyd Gaines, a black man who had tried unsuccessfully to enroll in the University of Missouri law school, which at that time only accepted white students. Since Missouri had no law school for black residents, the state offered him a partial scholarship to attend law school in another state. This was a common practice in southern states at the time.

The U.S. Supreme Court ruled that the State of Missouri had to provide Gaines with a law school education in Missouri that was as good as the education provided for whites or else admit Gaines to the state's all-white law school. After hearing one of New Haven's two black lawyers talk about the decision, young Constance made up her mind that one day she, too, would become a lawyer.

After graduating from high school with honors in 1939, Constance Baker got a job with the National Youth Administration, an agency that was established during the 1930s to help relieve unemployment among young people. Baker hoped to win a scholarship and to save enough money to begin college classes in a year or two. In the meantime, she attended lectures and classes at local community centers.

One evening, during a meeting at a community center in a black neighborhood, Constance Baker stood up and made a speech that changed her life. A wealthy white businessman, Clarence Blakeslee, was largely responsible for building the center to benefit the neighborhood residents. The center's directors—all of whom were white business and professional leaders—had called the meeting to find out why so few blacks took advantage of its programs.

Baker told the group that blacks did not come to the center very often because they had no voice in running it. The next day, Blakeslee asked to meet Baker. He liked her courage in speaking out before the group of community leaders, and he offered to finance her entire college education, including graduate study. Blakeslee knew that Baker had the ability to succeed in college since he had checked her high-school academic record before making his offer.

Baker chose to attend Fisk University in Nashville, Tennessee, one of the oldest black colleges in the United States. At Fisk, she met middle-class blacks whose parents were college-educated, and she learned firsthand about racial segregation in the South. (Although some New Haven restaurants served only whites, schools and most public facilities did not separate blacks from whites.)

Baker remained at Fisk from February 1941 until June 1942, when she transferred to New York University. After graduating from the university in October 1943 with a degree in economics, Baker was among the small group of women who entered Columbia University's law school. She received her law degree in August 1946.

During her last year in law school, Baker got a job that would profoundly affect the rest of her career. While working as a law clerk at the New York headquarters for the National Association for the Advancement of Colored People (NAACP), she did legal research for attorney Thurgood Marshall. Marshall was then chief counsel for the NAACP's Legal Defense and Educational Fund, which worked for racial justice through the courts. Marshall was impressed by his new law clerk's abilities,

In 1967, Thurgood Marshall (1908-1993) became the first African American appointed to the U.S. Supreme Court.

and he encouraged her by telling her about other successful African-American women.

Shortly after her law school graduation, Baker married Joel Motley, a former law student who had given up his law studies for a career in real estate and insurance. The couple had one son, Joel Motley Jr., who was born in 1952 and would eventually graduate from law school at Harvard University.

After Motley received her law degree, Marshall persuaded the NAACP to hire her on a full-time basis. This was a significant step for a black woman because at this time, as Motley later explained, African-American males were on the bottom rung of the professional ladder and "African-American women were not even on the ladder."

Constance Baker Motley, with her husband, Joel, and their son, Joel Jr.

One of Motley's first assignments as a lawyer for the NAACP was the case of Heman Sweatt, a black man who had tried unsuccessfully to enroll at the University of Texas law school in 1946. Instead of admitting Sweatt to the whites-only law school, the university's officials created a separate law school for Sweatt in a basement classroom, where he was the only student.

The NAACP lawyers argued that in this isolated classroom, Sweatt could not receive a legal education equal to that offered to white students. To prepare adequately for law careers, the NAACP argued, future lawyers needed the opportunity to meet with faculty members and discuss their ideas with other law students. In 1950, the U.S. Supreme Court agreed with this reasoning and held that the state of Texas had failed to provide Sweatt with a legal education equal to that provided for its white law school students.

During her years as a lawyer for the NAACP, Motley had a hand in most of the important cases during the civil rights movement. In fact, Motley helped attorney Thurgood Marshall write the arguments that he used in persuading the Supreme Court to rule in its landmark 1954 decision in *Brown v. The Board of Education of Topeka*. In a unanimous decision, the Court ruled that segregated school systems were inherently unequal and that they violated the Fourteenth Amendment's guarantee of equal protection under the law.

In 1950, after Linda Brown and 19 other black children in Topeka, Kansas, were not allowed to enroll in all-white public schools, the NAACP filed a discrimination suit on behalf of the students' parents.

Through her work for the NAACP, Motley helped to open state universities to black students in Alabama, Florida, Oklahoma, Georgia, and South Carolina. In addition, she represented black elementary school children in school segregation cases in a dozen southern states and three northern states. She also helped to free Martin Luther King Jr. and other civil rights leaders after the police arrested them during political protests.

One of Motley's best known cases involved a lengthy fight to get the University of Mississippi to admit a black student named James Meredith. In the autumn of 1960, Meredith, an air force veteran who had earned some college credits during his military service, enrolled in Jackson State College, a college for blacks that had been established in 1877. In January 1961, Meredith wrote to the University of Mississippi, a whites-only school, to request enrollment application forms. Meredith wanted to get a degree from *that* university, so he decided to tackle the issue of racial discrimination head on.

After receiving a friendly reply, Meredith returned the completed application with a letter informing the university that he was black. When the university promptly rejected his application for admission, Meredith filed a lawsuit in federal district court on behalf of himself and all others in a similar situation. In his lawsuit, Meredith

During the mid-twentieth century, segregated drinking fountains, buses, restaurants, and schools were common in the South.

claimed that the university had denied him admission solely because of his race.

The NAACP assigned Motley to Meredith's case. In choosing Motley to represent Meredith, the NAACP selected a lawyer who had all the necessary qualities to bring the case to a successful conclusion. Securing Meredith's admission to a whites-only school in Mississippi, a staunchly segregationist state, would require courage, determination, and careful preparation. The lawyer pleading Meredith's case would have to avoid giving the state of Mississippi an excuse for turning down his application for any reason other than his race.

In February 1962, the U.S. district court judge ruled in the university's favor. The judge held that the evidence showed that the university was not a segregated institution, even though it had never knowingly admitted a black student. Motley appealed the decision, and on June 25, 1962, after the state had employed numerous delaying tactics, the U.S. Court of Appeals for the Fifth Circuit reversed the decision of the district court.

In giving the reasoning behind the decision handed down by the appeals court, Judge John Minor Wisdom stated that once the university learned about Meredith's race, it engaged in "a carefully calculated campaign of delay, harassment, and masterly inactivity. It was a defense designed to discourage and to defeat by evasive tactics." Judge Wisdom observed that the university's actions appeared to be designed to defeat Meredith by

NAACP attorneys Constance Baker Motley and her colleague Jack Greenberg argued many cases before the U.S. Supreme Court.

putting up "discouragingly high obstacles that would result in the case carrying through his senior year." The university's delaying tactics failed to work only because, at Judge Wisdom's suggestion, Meredith had avoided graduation from Jackson State in the spring of 1962 by taking courses that would not lead to a degree.

Even after this decision by the U.S. Court of Appeals for the Fifth Circuit, Mississippi tried to stop Meredith from enrolling at the state university. At one point, Mississippi Governor Ross Barnett ordered all state officials to obey state laws instead of federal court orders. He described these orders as attempts to usurp the state's sovereign power.

When Meredith, accompanied by federal officials, arrived at the university in September 1962 to register for classes, an unruly white mob rioted on the campus. Before federal troops could restore order, two people were dead and hundreds of others were injured. Despite continual harassment during his student days, Meredith graduated from the University of Mississippi in August 1963.

As Motley worked for the NAACP in its court battles for racial justice, she gradually became convinced that court action was not the only solution for the problems black Americans faced during the 1960s. Court decisions could break down legal barriers in the South, but in the North, blacks faced other problems—poor housing, inadequate schools, and few job opportunities.

Motley was convinced that lawmakers, not judges, should address these problems. As she worked through her thinking on this issue, a black state senator resigned from the New York state legislature in February 1962 to become a judge. Seizing this opportunity, Motley won a special election to fill the vacancy. Thus, she became the first black woman to serve in the New York Senate. That November, she won a regular two-year term in the senate.

Motley did not complete her regular senate term, however. In February 1965, one of Motley's colleagues from the NAACP resigned as president of the Borough of Manhattan to become a judge. Following his resignation, the New York City Council elected Motley to fill the vacancy, making her the first woman to hold that office. In 1965, the voters elected her to a full four-year term as president of the Borough of Manhattan.

But once again, Motley did not complete her term of office. Early in 1966, President Lyndon Johnson named her as a judge on the U.S. District Court for the Southern District of New York, one of the busiest federal district courts in the United States. Many southern senators opposed Motley's nomination because of her previous court battles to desegregate southern schools.

One especially powerful opponent of Motley's nomination was Mississippi Senator James Eastland, an avowed segregationist. Eastland chaired the Senate Judiciary Committee, which voted on judicial appointments before the full Senate considered them. The

As part of his "Great Society" plan for the United States, President Lyndon Johnson (1908-1973), who served from 1963 to 1969, supported new civil rights legislation and new programs to help the poor.

senator from Mississippi blocked a Senate vote on Motley's appointment as long as he could. However, on August 24, 1966, the Senate finally confirmed her appointment.

On September 7, Judge Motley took the oath of office as the first black woman to serve as a federal judge. Of the more than 200 judges in the federal district courts at that time, only 3 of them—including Motley—were women. After serving as a federal judge for 16 years, Motley became "chief judge" of her district court in 1982. In 1986, she became a "senior judge," a term used to describe a retired judge who occasionally still hears cases.

Although Judge Motley overcame the barriers of race and gender to become a successful lawyer, elected official, and federal judge, she spent most of her energies fighting for racial justice. She herself once remarked, "I have been too busy eliminating discrimination against race to fight discrimination against women."

One of Motley's most important decisions as a senior judge, however, concerned the rights of women. In 1994, she ruled in favor of a female professor at Vassar College who claimed she had been denied tenure—a permanent position at the college—because she was married. Although Vassar (which is now co-ed) was the first women's college in the United States, Motley noted that during a 30-year period, Vassar had never given tenure to a married woman teaching in the "hard sciences," which include mathematics, biology, and computer science.

Motley said, "Vassar, despite its protest that it advances the cause of women, has consistently shown prejudice toward its married female faculty." Legal experts noted that this was the first case in which a judge found that a university had discriminated against women because they were married.

In an interview during the 1980s, Motley said that when she attended law school during the 1940s, civil rights had merited only a footnote in the textbooks, and legal scholars almost totally ignored women's rights at that time. In the decades since then, Motley has grown increasingly optimistic about the strides that women and minorities have made in the areas of politics and law.

By the end of her distinguished career, Patricia Roberts Harris (1924–1985) had held two cabinet positions and served as a U.S. ambassador.

8

Patricia Roberts Harris
Diplomat and Cabinet Member

*I*n April 1943, a small group of students at Howard University in Washington, D.C., protested at a local cafeteria that refused to serve blacks. One of the demonstrators was 18-year-old Patricia Roberts. Twenty years later, on August 28, 1963, Patricia Roberts Harris marched through the streets of the nation's capital in another peaceful protest. In this massive demonstration, thousands of Americans—both black and white—heard Martin Luther King's inspiring "I Have a Dream" speech about his hope for racial harmony.

Civil rights leader Martin Luther King Jr. (1929-1968) helped to organize the Montgomery bus boycott in 1954 and the 1963 March on Washington, D.C. He was awarded the Nobel Peace Prize in 1964.

Patricia Roberts Harris had come a long way in the years between 1943 and 1963. In that time, she earned a law degree and became a member of the faculty of Howard University's law school. She would go further still in the years ahead. First, to the tiny European country of Luxembourg as the first black woman ambassador from the United States, and then back to Washington, D.C., as the first black woman to hold a cabinet post.

Patricia Roberts was born on May 31, 1924, in Mattoon, Illinois, a mid-sized rural town. Her parents, Bert and Hildren Roberts (called "Chiquita"), were the descendants of slaves who had bought their freedom after moving from Virginia to Illinois. Now they were among Mattoon's few black residents.

Patricia learned about racial prejudice early in life. When she was in first grade, a white classmate taunted her with a racially offensive word. Later in life, that memory would contribute to her determination to do whatever she could to wipe out racial discrimination.

Patricia's father, who worked as a waiter on a railroad dining car, abandoned his family when Patricia was still a child. Chiquita Roberts later brought her two children, Patricia and Malcolm, to Chicago. As a single parent, Chiquita Roberts could give her children little in the way of material goods, but she did give them an appreciation of the value of an education. When Patricia graduated from high school, she received offers of scholarships from five colleges. She chose Howard University in Washington, D.C., one of the oldest and largest black colleges in the United States.

While she was a student at Howard, Patricia Roberts became vice-chair of the college chapter of the National Association for the Advancement of Colored People (NAACP). At that time, most public facilities in the nation's capital were racially segregated, as they were throughout the South. In April 1943, Roberts and other Howard students decided to force the issue. About two dozen of them ordered food at the Little Palace Cafeteria.

Even though this cafe was located in a black neighborhood, it served only white customers.

After the cafeteria employees refused to serve them, the students sat quietly at the restaurant tables. Alarmed at the prospect of seeing the seats filled with demonstrators instead of paying customers, the cafeteria management quickly announced a new policy of serving every customer, regardless of race. That experience taught

During the 1960s, many college students protested racial segregation by holding peaceful "sit-ins" at lunch counters where only whites were served.

Roberts the value of peaceful protest, a lesson she would remember for many years.

After graduating from Howard University in 1945 with highest honors, Roberts returned to Chicago. There, she did graduate study at the University of Chicago and worked as program director for the Chicago Young Women's Christian Association (YWCA). Returning to Washington, D.C., in 1949, she completed further graduate study at American University. While in the nation's capital, she also became assistant director of the American Council on Human Rights.

In 1953, Roberts became executive director of Delta Sigma Theta, a black sorority with national headquarters in Washington, D.C. She held this position until 1959. Roberts also became active in the Urban League, an organization that worked for racial justice and better living conditions for minorities. From 1953 to 1955, she chaired the welfare committee of the Washington, D.C., chapter of the Urban League.

In September 1955, Roberts married a Washington, D.C., judge named William Beasley Harris. With his encouragement, she enrolled in the George Washington University law school in 1957. There she combined her law studies with working as a research assistant and writing for the school's law review.

Continuing her civic activities during this period, Patricia Roberts Harris served on the executive board of the NAACP's District of Columbia chapter from 1958 to 1960. She also served on the board of directors of the YWCA's national organization from 1958 to 1959. In spite of her busy schedule, Harris ranked first in her class of 94 students when she received her law degree in 1960. She was also a member of the Order of the Coif, a national honor society for law students.

After receiving her law degree, Harris worked for the U.S. Department of Justice as an attorney in its criminal division. However, she did not stay long in that job. In the early 1960s, she resigned to become the first woman to teach at the Howard University law school. She held this part-time job while serving as associate dean of students at Howard University.

While working for the Justice Department, Harris had met U.S. Attorney General Robert Kennedy, who shared her commitment to ending racial discrimination. Remembering Harris's earlier work at the Justice Department, the attorney general persuaded his brother, President John F. Kennedy, to appoint Harris as co-chair of the National Women's Committee for Civil Rights in 1963. In this unpaid position, she encouraged women's groups to support civil rights bills in Congress.

After the assassination of President Kennedy on November 22, 1963, his successor, Lyndon Johnson, named Harris to the newly formed Commission on the Status of Puerto Rico. This Caribbean island had been a self-governing American *commonwealth* since 1952.

Soon after he was sworn in as president in 1961, John F. Kennedy (1917-1963) appointed his brother Robert as the U.S. attorney general.

While serving as attorney general from 1961 to 1964, Robert Kennedy (1925-1968) worked to guarantee blacks the right to register and vote in the South.

(Commonwealth status is an intermediate position between independence and statehood.)

The commission, composed of members representing both the United States and Puerto Rico, examined the question of the future relationship of the island with the United States. Would the Caribbean country become a U.S. state? An independent country? Or would Puerto Rico continue in its commonwealth status? In 1967, after the commission completed its work, the voters of Puerto Rico held an election to decide among these three options. They voted to continue as a commonwealth, a status that Puerto Rico still maintains.

Harris, an active member of the Democratic Party, was a delegate to the 1964 Democratic National Convention, where the delegates nominated Lyndon Johnson as a candidate for a full term as president. Harris gave a speech in support of his nomination during the convention. In 1965, President Johnson rewarded Harris for her work as both a member of a government commission and as a loyal Democrat by nominating her as the U.S. ambassador to the small European nation of Luxembourg. The Senate quickly confirmed the appointment.

The Senate's confirmation made Harris the first black woman to become a U.S. ambassador to a foreign country. After expressing her pride and gratitude over her appointment, the new ambassador remarked that the appointment made her a little sad, too. She was sad because, until that point, black women had never been considered for such appointments.

Harris showed that, even without experience as a professional diplomat, she could be successful as the head of a diplomatic mission to another country. The ambassador's personal qualities—warmth, intelligence, and a sense of humor—soon charmed the citizens of Luxembourg. Still, because Harris missed practicing law and teaching, she resigned as ambassador in September 1967 to return to law school at Howard University.

After coming home to the United States, Harris combined her duties as a full-time law professor with an appointment as an alternate delegate to the United Nations General Assembly. She also resumed her active participation in various civic groups.

In 1969, Professor Harris was named the dean of Howard University's law school. The post was another first for Harris, who became the first black woman to head an American law school. Her stay in this position was short and stormy, however. She had been on the job only two weeks when she had to deal with a complicated student protest, one of the countless protests that took place on U.S. college campuses during the late 1960s and early 1970s.

The student protesters refused to attend class unless Harris fired a professor they believed had unfairly failed several students. Harris, who thought the demand was unreasonable, tried to persuade the students to end their boycott and return to classes. She proposed that a committee of students and faculty members evaluate the list of grievances and recommend corrective action.

The protesters, however, said Harris was being uncooperative and seized the law school building, thus preventing students who had decided not to join the boycott from attending class. To remedy the situation, Harris called off her attempts to deal with the protesters and got a court order requiring them to leave the building. Angry and frustrated by the protest and other administrative issues affecting the university, Harris resigned after slightly less than one month on the job. She then joined a Washington, D.C., law firm.

During her years as a practicing lawyer, Harris remained a staunch Democrat. She headed the Credentials Committee during the 1972 Democratic National Convention, and she was a member of the Democratic National Committee from 1973 to 1976. Soon after Democratic candidate Jimmy Carter won the 1976 presidential election, he appointed Harris as the secretary of Housing and Urban Development (HUD). This made her the first black woman to hold a cabinet office.

While the Senate deliberated on her confirmation for the HUD appointment, one senator expressed concern that Harris, a successful lawyer, might not understand the problems that poor city residents faced. In her usual outspoken style, Harris replied, "I am a black woman, the daughter of a dining car waiter. . . . I didn't start out as a member of a prestigious law firm, but as a woman who needed a scholarship to go to school. If you think that I have forgotten that, you are wrong."

Impressed by Harris's speech, the Senate confirmed her appointment. As HUD Secretary, Harris spoke frequently about what she saw as the federal government's failure to deal adequately with the problems facing American cities. She stressed three factors: 1) weak local economies, 2) lack of jobs, and 3) housing discrimination. In May 1978, Harris maintained that the violence

While serving as president from 1977 to 1981, Jimmy Carter made more than 1,000 political appointments, and 12 percent of them went to African Americans.

and poverty that threatened so many areas of the world could in time spill over into U.S. cities as well.

In 1979, President Carter asked Harris to leave HUD for a post as secretary of the Department of Health, Education, and Welfare—now called the Department of Health and Human Services. Harris held that second cabinet post until 1981, when Carter left office.

In 1982, Harris made her first and only attempt to win elective office. That year, she ran for the Democratic nomination for mayor of Washington, D.C., against a black man named Marion Barry, who had served on the city council. As a wealthy and successful lawyer, Harris received the support of the city's middle-class voters. However, this group represented only a small minority of Washington, D.C., residents. Because of this, Harris received only 36 percent of the votes in the Democratic primary election. She lost to Barry, who campaigned as a champion of the city's poor residents.

After her loss in the 1982 primary, Harris returned to teaching and became a law professor at the George Washington University law school. She held that position until her death on March 23, 1985, which occurred shortly after her husband's death.

Like judge Constance Baker Motley, Patricia Roberts Harris devoted most of her efforts to eliminating racial barriers. Still, she believed that gender discrimination harmed U.S. society as much as racial discrimination. In a 1979 speech before the National Women's Political

At a 1979 press conference, Patricia Roberts Harris answers questions about her new position as secretary of Health, Education, and Welfare.

Caucus, she described her vision of the future of American women. Harris said:

> I want to hear the Speaker of the House addressed as Madam Speaker, and I want to listen as she introduces Madam President to the Congress assembled for the State of the Union. I want Madam President to look down from the podium at the women of the Supreme Court who will be indicative of the significant number of women judges throughout the Federal and State judicial systems.

Although more women have been appointed to important political positions since then, most of the events Harris envisioned in 1979 have yet to become reality. The woman closest to becoming president of the United States was Geraldine Ferraro, who in 1984 was the Democratic Party's vice-presidential candidate. But Ferraro and Democratic presidential candidate Walter Mondale lost that year's election in a landslide victory for the Republican incumbents, President Ronald Reagan and Vice-President George Bush. Nevertheless, the U.S. political system has moved a little closer to the ideal society that Harris described, where neither gender nor race disqualifies anyone from occupying a position of leadership.

Although vice-presidential candidate Geraldine Ferraro lost the 1984 election, many people consider her nomination a major political step for women.

In 1993, Ruth Bader Ginsburg became the 112th person—but only the second woman—appointed to the U.S. Supreme Court.

9

Ruth Bader Ginsburg
Supreme Court Justice

*R*uth Bader Ginsburg, the second woman appointed to the U.S. Supreme Court, almost missed becoming a member of the Court altogether. In early 1993, when Justice Byron White announced his retirement from the highest court, Ginsburg was serving as a judge on the U.S. Court of Appeals for the District of Columbia Circuit. When White retired, Ginsburg was among the small number of people whom President Bill Clinton initially considered for the job.

When Justice Byron White, who had been appointed to the Supreme Court in 1962 by President John F. Kennedy, announced his retirement 31 years later, President Bill Clinton had his first opportunity to appoint a Supreme Court justice.

Clinton, however, soon eliminated Ginsburg from consideration because he wanted to name someone with extensive political experience. Instead, he focused his attention on several prominent men, including Governor Mario Cuomo of New York, Education Secretary Richard Riley, Interior Secretary Bruce Babbitt, and Appeals Court judge Stephen Breyer. In June 1993, the president seemed to be on the verge of picking Judge Breyer. Instead, in a surprise announcement on June 14, he nominated Judge Ginsburg, calling her "one of our nation's best judges, progressive in outlook, wise in judgment, balanced and fair in her opinions."

Although President Clinton arrived at his decision by what one journalist described as "the messiest of paths," Judge Ginsburg proved to be a popular choice. She had been a women's rights lawyer for ten years before becoming a judge, and many legal scholars found her work on women's rights comparable to attorney Thurgood Marshall's work on racial justice for the NAACP.

Ginsburg had many political supporters, including Governor Ann Richards of Texas and Senator Daniel Patrick Moynihan of New York. Moynihan, in fact, told President Clinton that Ruth Bader Ginsburg was the best choice to fill the vacancy on the Supreme Court. In August 1993, despite some opposition from conservative groups, the U.S. Senate confirmed her appointment by an overwhelming majority, with only three senators voting against her confirmation.

Ruth Bader, the second of Nathan and Celia Amster Bader's two children (an older sister died at age six), was

Ginsburg answers questions during her Senate confirmation hearings.

born on March 15, 1933, in Brooklyn, New York. Nathan owned a small clothing store while Celia, who had worked in the garment industry before getting married, cared for their home and daughter.

Celia Bader, who died when Ruth was only 17, encouraged her daughter to be independent and to develop her abilities to their fullest extent. Ruth remembered that encouragement in later years. She once described her mother as "the bravest and strongest person I have known" and expressed the hope that "I may be all that she would have been had she lived in an age when women could aspire and achieve and daughters are cherished as much as sons."

After graduating from James Madison High School, Ruth Bader entered Cornell University in Ithaca, New York. During her freshman year, she met a pre-law student named Martin Ginsburg. The two were married in June 1954, shortly after Ruth's graduation, and she soon became pregnant with their first child, Jane.

Ginsburg's pregnancy gave Ginsburg firsthand experience with gender discrimination. The Social Security Administration had hired her for a technical job in one of its local offices in Oklahoma, while Martin Ginsburg was stationed there during his two years of military service. On learning about her pregnancy, the department demoted her to a clerical position. Ginsburg would later help to overturn provisions in the Social Security Act that discriminated against women.

After Martin Ginsburg finished his military service, the family moved to Cambridge, Massachusetts. There, Martin resumed his studies at Harvard University's law school, and Ruth enrolled as a first-year law student. She was 1 of only 9 women in a class of more than 500 students. The young parents led demanding lives because they had to fit child care, cooking, and other household chores into a busy schedule of classes and study. At times, Ruth Bader thought about dropping out of law school. However, she persisted in her studies, thanks to Martin's encouragement and his regular help with the housework.

After Martin Ginsburg obtained his law degree, the family moved to New York City, where Martin would become a successful tax lawyer. Ruth transferred to law school at Columbia University and received her law degree in 1959. But even though she and a classmate had tied for the top spot in their graduating class, Ruth had trouble finding a job as a lawyer. Ginsburg later said this was because she was both female and Jewish at a time when prominent law firms had only recently begun hiring significant numbers of Jewish men. Also, few law firms were hiring any women lawyers, especially mothers of young children.

Ginsburg's failure to find work with a New York law firm proved to be a blessing in disguise. Because she found no position in a city firm, she became a law clerk for a federal district court judge. This job gave her a thorough grounding in the operation of federal courts, and her two years of experience as a law clerk resulted in belated job offers from law firms. Ginsburg, however, decided to accept a position with Columbia's International Procedure Project. This new job involved living in Sweden on and off for two years while she studied the Swedish judicial system.

On her return from Sweden in 1963, Ginsburg taught at the Rutgers University law school in Newark, New Jersey, for nine years. During that period, she once again had to balance family and job responsibilities. When she became pregnant for the second time, Ginsburg did not want to risk losing another job because a child was on the way. So she hid the pregnancy by wearing oversize clothing. The timing of the pregnancy helped, too. Her son, James, was born in early September 1965. That meant that the later stages of Ginsburg's pregnancy, when it was almost impossible to hide, occurred during a summer vacation from Rutgers.

In 1972, after spending a year as a visiting professor at Harvard University's law school, Ginsburg joined the Columbia University law school faculty as its first woman professor with a permanent position. During this time, Ginsburg had become increasingly aware of the widespread gender discrimination in U.S. laws. To counter this, she began forming a strategy for fighting sex discrimination through the court system.

An active member of the American Civil Liberties Union (ACLU), Ginsburg was the principal author of the organization's legal argument, called a *brief*, for the case of *Reed v. Reed*, which reached the U.S. Supreme Court in 1971. The case involved Sally Reed, who asked to administer the estate of her adopted son after his death in 1967. The laws of Idaho, where the Reeds lived, gave priority to men over women in handling estates. Therefore, the state appointed Reed's husband, who was then separated from her, as the administrator of their son's estate.

Ginsburg argued that, by giving males preference over females when other factors were equal, the Idaho law violated the Fourteenth Amendment's guarantee of equal protection under the law. In 1971, a unanimous Supreme Court agreed with Ginsburg's argument and held the Idaho law unconstitutional. Some legal scholars have said that this landmark decision did for women what the *Brown v. The Board of Education of Topeka* school desegregation case had done for blacks. For the first time, the nation's highest court overturned a law in response to a woman's complaint of gender discrimination.

Shortly after the 1971 decision in *Reed v. Reed*, the ACLU formed a Women's Rights Project, with Ruth Ginsburg as its first director. In the next few years, she argued six gender discrimination cases before the U.S. Supreme Court and won five of them. As the NAACP had done in its racial discrimination lawsuits, Ginsburg and the other ACLU lawyers selected their cases carefully.

They helped men as well as women to fight discriminatory rules.

At this time in U.S. history, many laws were different for men and women. In her written briefs and oral arguments, Ginsburg tried to persuade the Court that these laws were the results of outdated ideas regarding the role of women in society. These laws dated back to a time when few women worked outside the home, Ginsburg pointed out, and the laws often assumed that women were dependent on their husbands for support and that men were more capable than women of making economic decisions. She argued that, by placing arbitrary limits on the roles of men and women, such laws were harmful to both.

Ginsburg presented her first oral arguments to the Court in 1972 in the case of *Frontiero v. Richardson*. Sharron Frontiero, a lieutenant in the air force, had applied for a housing allowance based on her marriage, an allowance that male officers received automatically. The air force, however, turned down her application and cited its rule that women officers could receive the allowance only if their husbands were dependent on them for support. In 1973, the Court held, by a majority of eight to one, that this gender-based difference in treatment violated the Fourteenth Amendment's equal protection clause.

Between 1973 and 1980, Ginsburg argued cases involving many different gender-based distinctions.

144

Within the Supreme Court building, the nine justices review lower-court decisions and decide whether existing laws are legal under the U.S. Constitution.

Perhaps the most important of these cases involved the rules regarding the rights of women to serve on juries. Many states, even after allowing women to serve on juries, made avoiding jury duty easier for women than for men. In 1961, a unanimous Supreme Court decision upheld a Florida law that allowed women to serve on juries only if they specifically asked to serve.

In delivering the 1961 opinion, the Court cited women's central role regarding the home and family. In the 1970s, thanks to Ginsburg's efforts, the Court issued two decisions reversing the 1961 position on this issue. In 1975, the Court struck down a Louisiana law excluding women from juries unless they had previously filed a written declaration of their desire to be subject to jury duty.

In 1979, the Court struck down a Missouri law that allowed women to decline jury duty without giving a reason. This gender-biased law, however, had said that men could avoid jury duty only under special conditions.

In 1980, President Jimmy Carter named Ginsburg to the U.S. Court of Appeals for the District of Columbia. During her 13 years on the appeals court, Ginsburg got along well with both her liberal and her conservative colleagues. A moderate, or centrist, in her judicial decisions, she generally looked for a common middle ground on which all the judges could agree. That may have been one of the reasons President Clinton nominated Ginsburg to the Supreme Court in 1993.

During his first few months in office, President Bill Clinton was often attacked for his political appointments, but few people objected when the president nominated Ruth Bader Ginsburg for the high court.

The Supreme Court following Ginsburg's appointment included (left to right) justices Sandra Day O'Connor, Clarence Thomas, Harry Blackmun, Anthony Kennedy, William Rehnquist (chief justice), David Souter, John Paul Stevens, Ruth Bader Ginsburg, and Antonin Scalia. In 1994, Stephen Breyer, whom President Clinton had considered appointing in 1993, joined the Court after Blackmun announced his retirement.

Justice Ginsburg's first opinion as a member of the Supreme Court showed her continued support for women's rights. The case of *Harris v. Forklift* dealt with a federal law protecting both men and women from sexual harassment on the job. Teresa Harris, who quit her job on October 1, 1987, because her employer continually made sexually explicit remarks and gestures at work, filed a lawsuit against her employer shortly afterward. In her suit, she claimed that her employer was guilty of illegal sexual harassment. A lower court ruled that, although her employer had used vulgar language, the employer had not violated the law because Harris had not suffered severe psychological damage as a result of his remarks.

In November 1993, a unanimous Supreme Court put aside the lower court's ruling. The highest court in the United States said that to win lawsuits based on sexual harassment in the workplace, employees do not have to prove that their work performance suffered as a result of their employers' behavior. Justice Sandra Day O'Connor, the first woman appointed to the Supreme Court, wrote the opinion for that decision.

During the oral arguments for the case of *Harris v. Forklift*, Justice Ginsburg had suggested that the conditions of employment are not equal for both sexes if one sex "is being called names and the other is not." Ginsburg then wrote a separate opinion agreeing with the unanimous decision of the Court. She proposed that as evidence of sexual harassment, employees need show only that an employer's behavior "made it more difficult to do the job."

In 1994, Justice Ginsburg had the opportunity to expand the right of both men and women to serve on juries. The 1994 decision, in which Ginsburg was part of a 6-3 majority, held that public prosecutors may not exclude potential jurors from serving solely because of their sex. The Court held that such an attempt to manipulate the makeup of the jury was a form of discrimination that perpetuated outmoded and overly broad notions regarding the relative abilities of men and women.

In a 1986 speech, Ruth Bader Ginsburg had described her ideal plan for achieving equal treatment for all Americans:

> First, it would promote equal educational opportunity and effective job training for women, so they would not be reduced to dependency on a man or the state. Second, my plan would give men encouragement and incentives to share more evenly with women the joys, responsibilities, worries, upsets, and sometimes tedium of raising children from infancy to adulthood. . . . Third, the plan would make quality day care available from infancy on. Children in my ideal world would not be women's priorities, they would be human priorities.

Justice Ginsburg's daughter, Jane Ginsburg Spera, now a law professor at Columbia University's law school, evidently shares her mother's dream of a society in which women are not restricted because of their reproductive functions. On learning of Ginsburg's nomination to the Supreme Court, Spera reminded her mother that upon graduation from high school in 1973, Spera's yearbook listed her ambition as "to see her mother appointed to the Supreme Court." The yearbook item then added, "If necessary, Jane will appoint her."

Important Women
In the Federal Government

In addition to the nine women profiled in this book, numerous other women have received important appointments in the federal government. Some of the best known among them are listed below.

- Eugenie Moore Anderson. b. 1909 in Adair, IA. Ambassador to Denmark (1949-1953) and Bulgaria (1962-1964).

- Clare Boothe Luce. b. 1903 in New York, NY. Ambassador to Italy (1953-1956). d. 1987.

- Oveta Culp Hobby. b. 1905 in Killeen, TX. Secretary of Health, Education, and Welfare (1953-1955).

- Frances Willis. b. 1899 in Metropolis, IL. Ambassador to Switzerland (1953-1957), Norway (1957-1961), and Ceylon (1961-1964). d. 1983.

- Shirley Temple Black. b. 1928 in Santa Monica, CA. Ambassador to Ghana (1974) and Czechoslovakia (1989).

- Carla Anderson Hills. b. 1934 in Los Angeles, CA. Secretary of Housing and Urban Development (1975-1977).

- Juanita Morris Kreps. b. 1921 in Lynch, KY. Secretary of Commerce (1977-1979).

- Shirley Mount Hufstedler. b. 1925 in Denver, CO. Secretary of Education (1979-1981).

- Jeane Kirkpatrick. b. 1926 in Duncan, OK. Ambassador to the United Nations (1981-1985).

- Margaret Heckler. b. 1931 in Flushing, NY. Secretary of Health and Human Services (1983-1985). Ambassador to Ireland (1985-1989).

- Elizabeth Hanford Dole. b. 1936 in Salisbury, NY. Secretary of Transportation (1983-1987) and Labor (1989-1990).

- Antonia Novello. b. 1944 in Fajardo, Puerto Rico. Surgeon General (1990-1993).

- Barbara Hackman Franklin. b. 1940 in Lancaster, PA. Secretary of Commerce (1992-1993).

- Sandra Day O'Connor. b. 1930 in El Paso, TX. Appointed to the Supreme Court in 1981.

- Madeleine Korbel Albright. b. 1937 in Prague, Czechoslovakia. Named Ambassador to the United Nations in 1993.

- Minnie Joycelyn Elders. b. 1933 in Schall, AR. Appointed Surgeon General in 1993.

- Hazel Reid O'Leary. b. 1937 in Newport News, VA. Named Secretary of Energy in 1993.

- Donna Shalala. b. 1941 in Cleveland, OH. Appointed Secretary of Health and Human Services in 1993.

Janet Reno, who was born in Miami, Florida, in 1938, became the first woman attorney general in 1993. She was one of the several women to receive major appointments in the federal government that year.

Bibliography

Addams, Jane. *My Friend, Julia Lathrop.* New York: Macmillan, 1935.

Allen, Florence Ellinwood. *To Do Justly.* Cleveland: Western Reserve University Press, 1965.

Anderson, Mary. *Woman at Work: The Autobiography of Mary Anderson, As Told to Mary N. Winslow.* Minneapolis: University of Minnesota Press, 1951.

Calkin, Homer L. *Women in American Foreign Affairs.* Washington, DC: Department of State, 1977.

Chamberlin, Hope. "In Search of an Image." *A Minority of Members: Women in the U.S. Congress.* New York: Praeger, 1973.

Cherny, Robert W. *A Righteous Cause: The Life of William Jennings Bryan.* Boston: Little, Brown and Company, 1985.

Coleman, Penny. *Breaking the Chains: The Crusade of Dorothea Lynde Dix.* White Hall, VA: Shoe Tree Press, 1992.

Davis, Michael D., and Hunter R. Clark. *Thurgood Marshall: Warrior at the Bar, Rebel on the Bench.* Secaucus, NJ: Carol Publishing Group, 1992.

Foner, Philip S. *Women and the American Labor Movement: From Colonial Times to the Eve of World War I.* New York: Free Press, 1979.

Gilbert, Lynn, and Gaylen Moore. *Particular Passions: Talks with Women Who Have Shaped Our Times.* New York: Clarkson N. Potter, 1981.

James, Edward T. *Notable American Women.* Cambridge: Harvard University Press, 1971.

Lamson, Peggy. *Few Are Chosen: American Women in Political Life Today.* Boston: Houghton Mifflin, 1968.

Lemons, J. Stanley. *The Woman Citizen: Social Feminism in the 1920s.* Urbana: University of Illinois Press, 1973.

Lowe, Corinne. "First Woman Diplomat." *Pictorial Review,* February 1934.

Marshall, Helen E. *Dorothea Dix, Forgotten Samaritan.* Chapel Hill: University of North Carolina Press, 1937.

Martin, George Whitney. *Madam Secretary: Frances Perkins.* Boston: Houghton Mifflin, 1976.

Mohr, Lillian Holmen. *Frances Perkins: "That Woman in FDR's Cabinet!"* New York: North River Press, 1979.

Murray, Pauli. *Song in a Weary Throat: An American Pilgrimage.* New York: Harper and Row, 1987.

Powledge, Fred. *Free at Last? The Civil Rights Movement and the People Who Made It.* Boston: Little, Brown and Company, 1991.

Roosevelt, Anna Eleanor, and Lorena A. Hickok. *Ladies of Courage.* New York: Putnam, 1954.

Stroup, Herbert. *Social Welfare Pioneers.* Chicago: Nelson-Hall, 1986.

Swiger, Elinor Porter. *Women Lawyers at Work.* New York: Messner, 1978.

Tobey, James A. *The Children's Bureau: Its History, Activities and Organization.* Baltimore: The Johns Hopkins Press, 1925.

Tuve, Jeannette E. *First Lady of the Law: Florence Ellinwood Allen.* Lanham, MD: University Press of America, 1984.

Whitney, Sharon, and Tom Raynor. *Women in Politics.* New York: Franklin Watts, 1986.

Index

Addams, Jane, 27, 39, 44, 45
alcohol, 22, *See also* Prohibition
Allen, Clarence, 90
Allen, Corinne Tuckerman, 90
Allen, Florence, Ellinwood, 97;
   as appeals court judge, 9, 88,
   89, 96, 98-102, 105; death of,
   102; decisions on TVA, 99,
   100-101; early years of, 90-
   92; as judge in state courts,
   95-96; as lawyer, 92-94; work
   for women's suffrage, 92-94
Allen, P. F., 6
Altgeld, John, 28
ambassadors, U.S., 6, 8, 9, 83,
   85, 87, 120, 122, 128-129
American Civil Liberties Union
   (ACLU), 142-144
American Council on Human
   Rights, 125
American Federation of Labor,
   47
American Medical Association,
   35
Anderson, Anna, 42, 43
Anderson, Hilda, 42
Anderson, Magnus, 42
Anderson, Mary: death of, 54;
   as director of Women's
   Bureau, 9, 40, 41, 50-54, 55;
   early years of, 42-43;
   immigration to U.S., 41, 42;
   and trade union movement,
   43-44, 46-47; and Woman in
   Industry Service, 49-50
Anderson, Matilda, 42
anti-Semitism, 67, 141
arbitration, 46, 47

attorney general, U.S., 8, 126,
   127, 151

Babbitt, Bruce, 138
Bader, Celia Amster, 139-140
Bader, Nathan, 139-140
Bader, Ruth, *See* Ginsburg,
   Ruth Bader
Baker, Constance, *See* Motley,
   Constance Baker
Baker, Rachel Huggins, 106
Baker, Willoughby, 106
Bangs, Edward, 13
Barnett, Ross, 116
Barry, Marion, 132
Beers, Clifford, 29, 30
Black, Hugo, 102
Blackmun, Harry, 147
Blakeslee, Clarence, 107-108
Brennan, William J., 102
Breyer, Stephen, 138, 147
Bridges, Harry, 68-70
British West Indies, 106
Brown, Linda, 112
*Brown v. The Board of Education
   of Topeka*, 111, 112, 143
Bryan, Mary Baird, 74
Bryan, Ruth, *See* Rohde, Ruth
   Bryan Owen
Bryan, Silas, 73
Bryan, William Jennings, 73-76,
   78, 87
Bush, George, 134

cabinet members, 8, 9, 53, 56,
   57, 64, 67, 71, 120, 122, 130-
   132
Cable Act, 80, 81

154

156

ABOUT THE AUTHOR

ISOBEL V. MORIN, a native of Patchogue, New York, got a "worm's eye" view of federal politics while working as a civil servant in the federal government. After retiring in 1985, she enrolled in graduate school at the University of Maryland in Baltimore County, where she received a master's degree in historical studies. Morin is also the author of *Women of the U.S. Congress* and *Women Who Reformed Politics*.

Photo Credits

Photographs courtesy of the Franklin D. Roosevelt Library: pp. 6, 58, 66, 84, 97 (both), 98; Library of Congress, pp. 10, 16, 18, 21, 24, 27, 30, 33, 35, 37, 46, 48, 50, 53, 62, 68, 69, 75, 79, 100, 103, 122, 127 (both), 131, 145, 146; The Bettmann Archive, pp. 15, 36, 40, 45, 124, 133, 135, 139; Schlesinger Library, Radcliffe College, pp. 31, 55; League of Women Voters of the United States, pp. 38, 93; Boston Public Library, Print Department, pp. 56, 71; Nebraska State Historical Society, pp. 72, 77; Minnesota Historical Society, p. 83; United Nations, p. 86; Western Reserve Historical Society, pp. 88, 99; Supreme Court Historical Society, pp. 102, 109, 136, 138, 147; Sophia Smith Collection, Smith College, pp. 104, 110, 115; Brown Foundation, p. 112; Mississippi Department of Archives and History, p. 113 (both); Lyndon Baines Johnson Library, p. 118; Bettye Lane Studio, p. 120; and U.S. Department of Justice, p. 151.